tempted
to leave
the cross

renewing the call
to discipleship

ERNEST R. FLORES

Foreword by Jeremiah A. Wright Jr.

JUDSON PRESS
PUBLISHERS SINCE 1824

VALLEY FORGE, PA

Library of Congress Cataloging-in-Publication Data

Flores, Ernest R.
    Tempted to leave the cross : renewing the call to discipleship / Ernest R. Flores.
— 1st ed.
    p. cm.
    ISBN-13: 978-0-8170-1524-4 (pbk. : alk. paper) 1. Jesus Christ—Crucifixion.
2. Theology of the cross. 3. Christian life. 4. Bible. N.T. Gospels—Criticism, interpretation, etc. I. Title.

    BT453.F56   2007
    248.4—dc22

                                                                    2007035081

Printed on recycled paper in the U.S.A.

First Printing, 2007.

To my dad

Contents

Foreword

When Dr. Leonard Sweet was president of the United Theological Seminary (a United Methodist school), he was commissioned by his denomination to do a study of denominational clergy. The report was to be presented at a United Methodist Annual Conference. The report was on the State of the Clergy on the cusp of the twenty-first century. There were several other clergy-scholars, local church pastors, and laypersons engaged in theological education on that commission. Their findings were so negative, however, that the bishops decommissioned the research group and refused to publish the report.

Nonetheless, Dr. Sweet edited the commission's findings, printed what he called "The Ladder or the Cross: The Plover Report" (now unauthorized), and shared it with those of us who were faculty and adjunct faculty at the United Theological Seminary.

The most dangerous (and painfully accurate) truth that the researchers uncovered was one that described Methodist clergy who enter the profession of pastoral ministry. It describes far too many clergy of every Protestant denomination that I have worked with over the past three decades. Dr. Sweet discovered that for many men and women who enter parish ministry, the primary symbol of the Christian faith—the cross—has been replaced by "the ladder." The ladder of success has supplanted the cross of our Savior.

What I am calling "the dangerous truth" is what Pastor Ernest Flores writes about in the following pages. Too many men and women in ministry no longer "cling to the old rugged cross." They are too busy trying to climb the ladder of success. Instead of sacrifice, self-denial, and faithfulness—the essence of the cross—their primary concerns involve self-care, self-fulfillment, and self-satisfaction.

Their focus is on "moving to the next level"—getting a larger church, building a bigger sanctuary, raising more money, landing a higher salary with better benefits, and gaining more prestige for their meager (and often trite) efforts. Instead of feeding the sheep, they are fleecing the flock where God has placed them—while feathering their own nests and keeping eyes and ears open for a better-paying position at a more prominent parish.

This "theology of the ladder" has the most devastating effect on the people of God—especially the people in the pews. Instead of denying self, serving others, and following the One who was wounded for our transgressions, too many people now see Christianity as a way of climbing that ladder, and they go to church looking for self-gratification and self-actualization.

Christians "shop around" for churches that speak to their needs, comfort them in their greed, and make them feel good about themselves. Across denominational lines, people in contemporary America are no longer looking for ministers of the gospel of Jesus Christ. They are looking for motivational speakers who show them how to get rich and get richer because, after all, "you only go around once!"

Somewhere in this mad dash to climb the ladder, the message of Jesus of Nazareth who died on the cross gets completely lost. Christians who fall into this trap—led by the clergy!—are no longer concerned about the ones whom Jesus called "the least of these." We are no longer interested in addressing social justice issues such as racism, sexism, homophobia, an illegal war, legalized torture, the governmentally sanctioned murder of civilians, the lies of governmental officials, genocide in Sudan, and the Israeli-Palestinian question. In fact, because of the ladder theology being preached, people in the pews now see those issues as not being "religious."

The cross of Christ has been removed from sanctuaries and "worship centers," and also from the thoughts, the minds, and the hearts of men and women who flock to these "ladder gospel" preachers. The words of Jesus who said, "If anyone would come after me, let them deny themselves and pick up their cross" get lost in this new-fashioned religion. The hymn "Must Jesus Bear the Cross Alone?" gets dropped from the repertoires of choirs and congregations. Even more tragically, the notion of cross-bearing goes missing entirely from the theological understanding of what it means to follow the One who bore the cross of redemption to Calvary.

Even those preachers who *do* "preach Christ and him crucified" tend to focus exclusively on the vertical arm of the cross, which represents the believer's relationship with God, neglecting the horizontal arm of the cross, which represents our relationships with those who live in God's world beside us. This horizontal arm addresses those issues and areas of life where our faith is connected to the social justice issues that daily confront the people who sit in the pew. For those pastors who have succumbed to the temptation to leave the cross, there is no such "horizontal" content in their sermons. That is where the laity are most damaged—spiritually, theologically, sociologically, and psychologically. Church members are led astray by false shepherds, and women and men then pass on the "disease of disconnect" to their children and to their children's children.

It is precisely at this juncture that the reflections and scholarship of Pastor Ernest Flores are critical and crucial! He speaks to this sad condition in Christianity and offers us, lay and clergy alike, the tools for changing the course of the "Old Ship of Zion," which is headed for the rocks of heresy and total destruction. Pastor Flores not only resists the temptation to leave the cross of Calvary, but he also echoes Jesus' call for us to bear our own crosses, each and every day of our lives.

You will be blessed by this book. You will be engaged by this minister's brilliant mind. You will be challenged by his messages. As a disciple of Jesus, you will come away from the reading of this text with tools to take up the Cross of Jesus and to follow the one who leads us to life more abundant and to life eternal! These words challenge clergy and laity alike to do as the apostle Paul said: to "examine yourself." If you take Pastor Flores's wrestlings with the Scripture seriously, I guarantee that you will be changed by the time you get to the last chapter of this work.

Reverend Dr. Jeremiah A. Wright Jr.
Senior Pastor
Trinity United Church of Christ
Chicago, Illinois

Acknowledgments

Thanks to Jesus Christ for saving my soul—and my family's history! "If it had not been for the Lord. . . ."

To my beautiful wife, Deborah, for inspiring me, holding me accountable, partnering with me, challenging me, and being the best friend anyone could ever be. To my children, Armida and Rachel, for providing me with love and joy. To my mother, Armida C. Flores, who exemplifies Christ for me and whose expectations beckon me higher.

To the preacher-mentors who have advised and set a standard for proclaiming the gospel: Rev. Donald Grant, Dr. Jesse Miranda, Dr. Isaac Canales, Rev. Ray Mesa, the late Dr. S. Howard Woodson, Rev. Raimundo Jiminez, the late Rev. Roberto Fiero, the late Bro. Louie Millan, Bro. Ralph Alfaro, Dr. DeForest Buster Soaries, Dr. Jeremiah A. Wright Jr., Dr. G. Daniel Jones, Rev. Pablo Calzoncit, and my tios, the late Rev. Isaias Flores, Rev. Elias Flores Sr., the late Rev. Eliseo Flores, and Rev. Clemente Sanchez, and of course, my dad, Rev. Aureliano P. Flores.

To the Second Baptist Church of Germantown, which has supported my ministry and encouraged my growth. To our church secretary, Dot Kelly, our faithful friend for many years. And to my home church, Church of the Redeemer, especially Emma Alfaro, Tia Rachel Flores, Sis. Mary Robles, and Tia Annie Garcia.

To my colleagues who have wrestled together with me over Scripture while having breakfast or navigating a local golf course: Rev. Arlington Medley, Rev. Cean James, Dr. Bruce Alick, Dr. Alyn Waller, and Rev. Leonard Dow.

And to Rebecca Irwin-Diehl and the staff at Judson Press who helped me to proclaim Christ by this means.

Introduction

The preaching of the cross was something that my father, Rev. Aureliano Flores, did with regularity. Fixed in the deepest parts of my memory is my uncle Dickie Chavez leading our congregation, the Church of the Redeemer, in singing the old *corito* "En la Cruz."

Somewhere along the way, as I developed my own preaching and pastoral ministry, the cross of Jesus gave way to make room for more contemporary homiletical themes. But a few years ago I read an article about Billy Graham in which he was asked about how his preaching had changed as he had grown older. Rev. Graham answered, "I preach more about the cross than I used to." Sometime thereafter, I was installed as the pastor of the First Baptist Church of Ridgefield Park, New Jersey, my first pastorate. My pastor from Trenton, Rev. Dr. S. Howard Woodson Jr., came to preach the sermon, and the title of his sermon that evening was "Tempted to Leave the Cross." And like everything Dr. Woodson preached, that sermon penetrated my heart. It convicted me of failing to preach in a substantive manner what Jesus had done for us on the cross of Calvary, and it called into question why I was so obsessed in my preaching with trendy material matters instead of salvation matters.

And not just me, for it seems that many of us have gone after a Christianity based on the motto "What God can do for you and your situation." We have become more American in our consumeristic obsession than we are like Jesus and his suffering servanthood. Some of my colleagues and I have identified what we refer to as "victory theology," in which the focus on God and Christ is essentially for the purpose of gaining the victory for ourselves. Healings, miracles, jobs, financial prosperity—the whole "health and wealth" gospel—all of it is based on the idea that God is really God only if we are victorious. And we struggle to become anything like the Jesus who "laid down his life for his friends." And we certainly fail to lead anybody else to become like him.

What has happened to me in preaching the cross as often as I can these past few years is the effect of making myself and the members of my church more grateful for our salvation, more willing to share our wonderful Jesus with others because of our certainty of his great love for humanity. We are more service-conscious than blessing-conscious. There is a humility that comes from such a concerted focus on what Jesus did, and a heightened sense of what it means to be a Christian, to take up one's cross and follow him. The possessions and the blessings that are so associated with today's popular Christianity are rendered incredibly pale in comparison to the sacrificial effort made by our Lord. And I am ashamed of myself to think that I, as a preacher, have preached so often about what Jesus can do for us without depicting with any real power what Jesus *has done* for us.

Christ has been everything to me; that is certain. Raised in a Christian home, graduated from college and seminary, married to a wonderful wife, blessed with two healthy children, pastor of a loving congregation, I have been truly blessed by my Lord. I can't imagine what I'd be without him. Yet, these days when I sing the old song "What He's Done for Me," it isn't so much the blessings of my family and education and vocation that come to mind. Instead, it is the sufferings, beatings, and injuries that Christ endured and his blood shed for my sins so that I might be reconciled to God. That's "What He's Done for Me." Nothing material could compare to that. No other blessing is as valuable or should be as treasured.

It is my prayer that this book of sermons will inspire us all once again to be cross-centered, to value the high price that Jesus paid for our salvation, and to compel us to be selfless and sacrificial in our Christianity.

A View to the Cross
(Isaiah 53)

He was wounded for our transgressions, crushed for our iniquities; upon him was the punishment that made us whole, and by his bruises we are healed. (Isaiah 53:5)

One morning, I was expecting an important phone call. When the phone rang, I jumped to answer it with my customary "Hello, this is Rev. Flores." But it wasn't the person I was expecting, and I didn't recognize the voice that replied, "Hello, Rev. Flores." So I asked, "Who is this?" And the voice came shouting at me, "Hey, it's your mama!" We laughed at how I was so busy that I didn't even recognize my own mother's voice, but she told me that I didn't recognize her voice because I wasn't expecting it. Had I some form of expectation, I might have recognized her. When I told my wife about the incident and my mother's take on it, she said, "Either that or you could just start checking the caller ID like I've been telling you."

It is often controversial in theological and ecclesiastical circles to suggest of this writing by the Jewish prophet Isaiah that it speaks of Jesus. But it's Jesus that I, as someone reared in the Christian tradition, am expecting to see when I read this passage. As a historian and theologian, I am intrigued about the identity of the person that Isaiah had in mind when he wrote these magnificent and distressing words about a suffering servant upon whom the Lord had laid the iniquity of us all.

Who Is the Suffering Servant?

Isaiah wrote long before the time of Christ, and so obviously he had no firsthand knowledge of who Jesus was. Mel Gibson, in the first image of his film *The Passion of the Christ,* quotes the last phrase from Isaiah 53:5.[1] Beneath the Scripture he inscribed "701 B.C.," causing biblical scholars everywhere to squirm in their seats, knowing that the date was entirely debatable. In any case, it was several centuries before Jesus was born, and many people believe that Isaiah must have been referring to someone other than Jesus at some other time in history. Indeed, the people of God had looked for a deliverer on many occasions, and in 721 B.C. the northern kingdom of Israel had been attacked, defeated, and crushed by the Assyrian Empire, and the people of God at that time were in need of a deliverance that never did come for the ten lost tribes of Israel. About 125 years after that historic episode, the people of the southern kingdom of Judah came under attack from the Babylonian Empire, and they too were defeated in battle and were in need of a savior.

It is difficult enough for scholars to understand about whom Isaiah was speaking when he wrote so often and so eloquently about the long-awaited messiah. Was there some figure dealing with the northern kingdom in the 700s of which the prophet spoke, so that God might deliver his people from Assyrian oppression? And if Isaiah was to have written concerning the Babylonian Empire and the deliverance of the people of Judah, how could he do so from a distance of well over one hundred years? Indeed, the prophecies of Isaiah are so detailed that they mention the name of the Persian king who would conquer Babylon and send the people of God home to rebuild their city and temple. But how could Isaiah, writing well over a century earlier, have known that it would be Babylon that God would use to discipline his people, and that it would be Persia that would rise up and defeat Babylon to set God's people free, and that the name of the Persian king who would set them free would be "Cyrus"?

Hence the controversy, which leads some to believe that there were at least two prophets who wrote under the name "Isaiah," and that those prophets lived at historically different times and therefore knew the names of the characters involved in the story of God's discipline and deliverance of his people.

Simple enough, but when I read that text, when I read about this suffering servant, when I read how the Lord has laid upon him the iniquity of us all, my question is not about Cyrus or Babylon or anything like that. I want to know how Isaiah, writing several centuries before the time of Christ, described in such vivid detail what Jesus preached, suffered, and performed for us. These words of the prophet Isaiah seem to have reached out across the centuries and depicted with great precision the meaning and means of the death of Jesus, the passion of the Messiah. How did Isaiah do that? How did he understand so clearly that "he was despised and rejected by others" (Isaiah 53:3)? Did Isaiah sit in the courtyard while the people shouted, "Give us Barabbas!"? Was he there when the high priest declared to Pilate, "We have no king but Caesar"? Did he have some type of out-of-body experience that enabled him to time-travel across those centuries and see the crowd yelling, "Crucify him!"? What else could have compelled him to write the words "He was despised and rejected by others"? Could the prophet Isaiah, in some way beyond our poor powers of understanding, have seen Jesus?

Then, Isaiah said that this servant "was a man of suffering and acquainted with infirmity" (Isaiah 53:3).

Now, my understanding of human nature is that we tend to want our heroes to be of a certain ilk. Success and strength should ooze from their character. Their personality must convey an air of confidence and of knowledge, of justice and of peace, of goodness and trustworthiness. That's who we want our leaders to be. And Isaiah wrote of the messiah along those lines—powerful, good, just, regal, peaceful. Not here, in Isaiah 53, but earlier, where "the government will be upon his shoulder, and his name will be called 'Wonderful Counselor, Mighty God, Everlasting Father, Prince of Peace'" (Isaiah 9:6 RSV). That's a potent and venerable line of thought that Isaiah preached eloquently. But here in Isaiah 53:3 the messiah is not depicted as a regal figure, a praiseworthy noble.

The prophet seems to have witnessed not a man having that air of invincibility, but rather a man of suffering and acquainted with infirmity. Things don't always work out the way this suffering servant would want them to. Not every desire of his came to pass. He is accustomed to not getting his way from time to time. It is as though Isaiah was there in the garden of Gethsemane, witnessing firsthand when Jesus prayed, "Father, if you are willing, remove this cup from me; yet, not my will but yours be done" (Luke 22:42). A man acquainted with infirmity, a man of suffering—I've just seen Jesus. In this ancient manuscript, in this prophetic voice, in this prose and poetry, I've just seen Jesus.

There are versions of Christianity that shun the concept of a suffering servant. They would worship only a powerful king who gives us authority over demons, who casts out evil spirits, who miraculously cures incurable diseases. And, as we saw, Isaiah depicted that image of the messiah. And, truth be told, I'm a living witness that God can do anything but fail. I've cried unto the Lord, and he has heard my cry. I know the Lord as a healer and as a burden bearer. God has made a way for me. But let me warn you about something: when Christianity loses its servanthood, when it loses its humility, when we lose our ability to be acquainted with grief, to be people of suffering, then we lose the centrality of the cross of Jesus. And when we lose the centrality of the cross of Jesus, we lose our need to be redeemed and forgiven of our sins, and thus we lose our salvation. Christianity is not a "get rich quick" scheme. Christianity is not a means of keeping up with the Joneses. Christianity is not a chauvinistic strategy for global domination. No, Christianity at its core and at its best is a suffering servant, a man of sorrows, acquainted with infirmity.

Our nation is enamored with politicians born into wealth and power, people who had others pulling strings for them, doing underhanded things to keep them from having to live like everyone else. The same is true of our religion. We want a "health and wealth" gospel instead of understanding that anyone who wants to be greatest must be a servant. We want a "name it and claim it" theology instead of praying to God, "Not my will but yours be done." We want that. But centuries before it occurred, Isaiah looked through the window of history, and somehow he must have seen Jesus, a man of suffering and acquainted with infirmity.

I was a reluctant viewer of Mel Gibson's *The Passion of the Christ*. There was a part of me that didn't want to see what I imagined would be there. Sure, I had done what many of us do with words of Scripture that are too discomforting to contemplate. I had read that Jesus was scourged, whipped, beaten; that a crown of thorns was placed on his head. I had read and sung countless times about the nails driven through his hands and feet. But somehow, the reality of those words had been packed away in some storage container in the dark recesses of my mind, so that to genuinely consider what Jesus endured, how he truly suffered, was something that I didn't really want to do.

For me, going to the theater that day was like getting in line for a rollercoaster. My nerves were jangled about what I knew was coming up, but once was I was on board, I was powerless to stop it. Some of us have in fact contemplated the real meaning of those words—scourge, whip, thorns, nails—and we've decided that we don't deal well with violence and don't want to see it. Indeed, as I watched Gibson's interpretation of some of the horrible things that were inflicted on our Lord, it was difficult to keep my eyes on the screen. I wanted to turn my head away. I wanted to look away from his deep suffering. Gibson even has characters who turn their faces away from the gore of this tortured, condemned man—parents shield their children from the gruesome sight of Jesus dying for you and me. I wonder how Isaiah understood all that from a distance of half a millennia, when he spoke of "one from whom others hide their faces" (Isaiah 53:3). Somehow, he must have just seen Jesus.

How did Isaiah see all that? Was he within earshot somehow from his perspective of several centuries so that he noticed how "He did not open his mouth; like a lamb that is led to the slaughter, and like a sheep that before its shearers is silent, so he did not open his mouth" (Isaiah 53:7)? Was Isaiah there among the crowd before the high priest Caiaphas or in the courtyard before Pilate when he wrote, "By a perversion of justice he was taken away. Who could have imagined his future?" (Isaiah 53:8)? How did Isaiah know that "he was numbered with the transgressors" (Isaiah 53:12), one on his left and one on his right? And how did Isaiah see that "they made his grave with the wicked and his tomb with the rich" (Isaiah 53:9)? These events were recorded in the Gospel accounts hundreds of years later. I've just seen Jesus in a prophetic writing penned centuries before his birth.

Who Causes the Servant to Suffer?

Let's move to the verse where Isaiah prophetically wrote, "Surely he has borne our infirmities" (Isaiah 53:4). Surely. No doubt about whose infirmities they were. They were ours.

When *The Passion of the Christ* was first released, controversy erupted in charges of anti-Semitism against the film and against Mel Gibson. The statement "The Jews killed Jesus" was something I hadn't heard until adulthood, but historically it's been understood to mean that one group of people was solely responsible for the death of Jesus on the cross. Some religious leaders point the finger elsewhere, saying that it wasn't the Jews who killed Jesus but rather the Romans—as if that makes it any less a racist statement. That view only changes which race to blame; it doesn't eliminate the racism. And that is so typical of human beings: shift the blame from ourselves to others, deflect criticism, pin the rap on somebody else.

So much hatred has been heaped on the Jewish people by folks failing to acknowledge what Isaiah so clearly understood from his vantage point preceding the events of the cross: it wasn't the Jews who killed Jesus. Surely he bore *our* infirmities. Surely. Make no mistake about it: "All we like sheep have gone astray; we have all turned to our own way, and the LORD has laid on him the iniquity of us all" (Isaiah 53:6). Isaiah 53:8 says, "He was cut off from the land of the living, stricken for the transgression of my people." Isaiah 53:10 says, "It was the will of the LORD to crush him with pain. When you make his life an offering for sin, he shall see his offspring, and shall prolong his days; through him the will of the

LORD shall prosper." And in the next verse, "The righteous one, my servant, shall make many righteous, and he shall bear their iniquities" (Isaiah 53:11). And in the latter part of Isaiah 53:12 it says, "Yet he bore the sin of many, and made intercession for the transgressors." I don't know about you, but I've just seen Jesus. "He was wounded for our transgressions, crushed for our iniquities; upon him was the punishment that made us whole, and by his bruises we are healed." I've just seen Jesus.

Seeing Jesus

I no longer see Jesus the way I used to see him. I don't see Jesus in people who call his name but never turn the other cheek.

I don't see Jesus in those who have time to worship but who have no capacity to forgive.

I don't see Jesus in those who are more concerned with preserving their dignity than with developing their servanthood.

I don't see Jesus in politicians who use him as a reelection tool and then discard his love of enemies as soon as our enemies appear.

No, but I do see Jesus in the sacrificial giving of saints to ensure the proclamation of the gospel message.

I see Jesus when saints of God deny themselves and reach out into the community to help those who are less fortunate.

I see Jesus in those who provide shelter for the homeless and meals for the poor.

I see Jesus when the church suffers with those who suffer, when we're weeping with those who are weeping, mourning with those who are mourning.

I see Jesus in the humility of the cross, in the suffering servant Messiah giving his life as a ransom for many. And when I read Isaiah 53, I've just seen Jesus.

Cross Examinations

1. What are your expectations of a savior, and how does Jesus fulfill them?
2. How has God been made real in your life?

3. How do you handle the contradictions of Jesus (servanthood and power, peace and suffering, his will and my will)?

4. Who are the people in whom you see Jesus? Can others see Jesus in you today?

Note

1. *The Passion of the Christ*, directed by Mel Gibson (20th Century Fox, 2004).

You Just Don't Get It
(Mark 10:32-45)

Jesus said to them, "You do not know what you are asking. Are you able to drink the cup that I drink, or be baptized with the baptism that I am baptized with?" (Mark 10:38)

Jesus went into the grim details about how he was going to be killed, killed for the sake of the entire world. In the midst of that passionate description of what he most greatly feared, James and John essentially interrupted and said, "Excuse me, Lord, but can we sit on your right and on your left when you ascend the throne in Jerusalem?" Jesus probably was a bit perturbed when he said to them, "You don't know what you're asking for," but I think that what he meant was, "You just don't get it."

Consider a married couple, one of whom has been pouring out soul-baring feelings and thoughts on matters of the heart to the other, and the spouse responds, "Sure, honey, but can't this wait until the commercial break?" Or think about the teacher who has studied, organized lessons, prepared lectures, and developed innovative ways of teaching young people, only to find a student at the final exam who doesn't even know what the subject is. After a Sunday school class, a teacher gave a fill-in-the-blank test to the young students to see if they understood the lesson. The first question was, "_____ your enemies." One student supplied "Punch." Another offered "Run from." Another chose "Pants." You just don't get it, do you? Come to think of it, the

9

same teacher could have given the same test to some of our government leaders, and they might well have come up with "Preemptively strike your enemies," or "Go to war against your enemies," or "Arrest and sexually humiliate and degrade your enemies." Some of them are Bible-carrying Christians too, but when it comes to remembering what Jesus said about loving your enemies, they just don't get it.

James and John had spent months and months with Jesus, eating with him, traveling with him, asking him questions, and listening to his teachings, and still they failed to grasp what he was about. There are folks who go to church every Sunday. On Saturday, they'll spend a lot of time and money at the barbershop or beauty salon, the clothing and shoe stores, working all day long to get just the right look. And the next day they go to church, sing and shout, and have themselves a good ol' time. But ask them what the sermon was about, and they just don't get it. Ask them to quote a Scripture, any Scripture, and they just don't get it. Ask them why they go to church on Sunday morning and sing like an angel but then go to bars on Friday night and lie like the devil: "No, I'm not married. I'm only twenty-five years old." They just don't get it. Going to church Sunday after Sunday, hearing about Jesus week after week, but they just don't get it.

Jesus was talking about service and sacrifice, but James and John were interested in power and prestige. Jesus was talking about the least of these, but they were concerned about being the greatest of these. Jesus was preaching about God's ways, but they were interested in getting their own way. Jesus was praying that God's will be done, but they were asking for personal favors. They just didn't get it.

Have you ever known someone like that? Have you ever worked with or been married to someone like that? Even more disturbing, have you ever *been* someone like that? That's the question we really need to ask ourselves, because it's easy for anyone to look at these disciples and note how they had totally missed out on Jesus' message and purpose. But the fact is that a whole lot of us are doing the exact same thing. There are a whole lot of folks going to church who don't love their enemies. There are a whole lot of folks who have their names on the membership roll, but the only time they turn the other cheek is when they're on an uncomfortable mattress! And if we're honest, if we're really looking to improve our own spiritual lives, if we're really trying to be more like Jesus and thereby make the world a better place, then we'll take time right now to consider these disciples and their misunderstanding of Jesus so that we can grasp some of the things that lead a follower of Jesus—*any* follower of Jesus—to miss out on his meaning and message.

Prioritizing Personal Ambition

When your primary concern is personal ambition, you just don't get it. James and John said to Jesus, "Teacher, we want you to do for us whatever we ask of you" (Mark 10:35). We live in a culture that encourages us to insist on having it our way, to get what we want when we want it, no matter who gets hurt in the process. Christianity has been the dominant religion of the Western world for more than fifteen hundred years. Yet, it is the Western world that gave us the slave trade. It is the Western world that gave us colonialism. It is the Western world that gave us Manifest Destiny. It is the Western world that gave us the Holocaust. It is the Western world that has given us war after war after war. And each of these atrocities was based on the notion of one people getting whatever they want, pursuing their own ambition with no regard for the humanity and existence of anyone else, with no regard for what Jesus said and did. All the while, the Western world is worshiping on Sundays, using Christ's name during election season, building grand cathedral after grand cathedral, opening sessions of Congress with prayer, and fighting about prayer in schools and the Ten Commandments in public venues. We just don't get it.

In the movie *The Godfather: Part III*, a priest takes a stone out of a pool of water and cracks it open, revealing that the inside of the stone is still dry. He says, "For centuries, the Western world has been surrounded by Christianity, yet Christ has not penetrated our hearts."[1] So here's Jesus, graphically describing the passion that he would experience for the sins of the world, and the first words out of the mouths of James and John were, in essence,

"Give me whatever I want." They didn't say, "Forgive me, Lord, for my violence in thought and deed." Instead, they made a request for fame. They didn't say, "Thank you, Lord, for taking the penalty for my sins." Rather, they asked to become a household name. They didn't say, "Change my heart, Lord, so that I too might lead by serving, so that I too might demonstrate that it is more blessed to give than to receive, so that I too might change the world one person at a time by becoming a servant."

These two disciples are emblematic of personal ambition run amok, of the obsession that the present generation has with the word "more"—more money, more power, more houses, more toys . . . more, more, more. We want what we want, and we want it right now. So even when Jesus offers us a vivid image of what he has done for us, how great a servant he is, how marvelous is his love for humanity, we still manage to barrage him with requests that are self-centered instead of Christ-centered. We pray prayers that mention our desires and goals and ambitions, and that are devoid of requests for *God's* desires, goals, and ambitions for our lives and our church and our society. "I want to sit beside you on your throne in your kingdom. I want to be a powerful person. I want to have people know who I am, respect me, bow down before me." When you're consumed with personal ambition, whether or not you've been going to church, whether or not your name is on the membership roll, whether or not you're a deacon or a choir member or even a preacher, Jesus says that you don't know what you are asking, because you just don't get it.

Accepting Society's View

When you are accepting society's view of things rather than God's view, you just don't get it. Look at how James and John said it: "Grant us to sit, one at your right hand and one at your left, in your glory" (Mark 10:37). I mentioned in chapter 1 how the Jewish people of that day were indeed looking for a savior. At that time, they were living under Roman occupation, the Romans having succeeded the Greeks, who had conquered Judea a few centuries earlier under Alexander the Great. At the time of Jesus, the Jewish people had already been living under occupation by foreign invaders for centuries. They had not known autonomy and freedom as a people, and they were thirsting for a savior, a deliverer, a Moses-like leader who would come and throw off the yoke of Roman oppression and foreign occupation and liberate the people of God. It is highly likely that every time the disciples of Jesus mentioned his kingdom or his glory, they were referring to his leading a revolt against Rome and establishing a Jewish state over which they would be leaders. "Let us sit by your side when you come into your kingdom." "When will you restore to us the kingdom?" "Tell us what will be the signs of the coming of your kingdom." They were interested in an earthly, nationalistic kingdom that would resemble modern-day nations and administrations. They were asking for this because that was the prevailing understanding of how they were going to be redeemed and liberated. Society—well-intentioned and well-meaning society—was of the opinion that it was only right to think that a violent, military overthrow of foreign occupation was what to expect from a savior or a messiah.

Well, as we know, every now and then society gets it wrong. Every once in a while the will of the people isn't the will of God. Every now and then public opinion polls conflict with the word of God. So-called free love turned out to have all kinds of hidden costs, such as teen pregnancy, sexually transmitted diseases, and low self-esteem. It turns out that free love is actually way too expensive. Every now and then society gets it wrong. Getting high has been in vogue for quite a while now, but it's actually like jumping out of an airplane without a parachute—it will end your life. Drug addiction, rehab clinics, lost jobs, wrecked marriages, jail time—these are the hidden costs of shooting up and checking out. And just because everybody's doing it doesn't mean that God approves of it. Just because your friends are doing it, just because you're expected to do it, just because every movie and every TV show has pretty people who are doing it doesn't make it right.

You're going to hear a lot of things that society says are all right but that God says are all wrong. And you'll have to ask yourself, "Whom am I going to serve?" Because, as Bob Dylan put it in one of his songs, "You're gonna have to serve somebody." You'll either serve this world, which wants you to experiment with drugs, engage in promiscuous sexual behavior, and make as much money as you can legally or otherwise, or you'll serve the Lord Jesus Christ and become a servant to all. You'll either serve the almighty dollar or you'll serve the almighty God. You'll either serve the dealer and drugs or you'll serve the Healer and Judge. But make no mistake about it: you're going to serve *somebody*. You may not think about it that way, but you're serving some-body right now. You're following somebody right now. And it doesn't matter if you're in church, or if your name is on the mem-bership roll, or if you're wearing a nice dress or suit; if you're accepting society's view of things instead of God's view, then you just don't get it.

Exalting Self-Regard

Not only when you are concerned primarily with personal ambi-tion or when you accept society's view of things, but also when you regard yourself too highly, you just don't get it. Jesus says to James and John, "You do not know what you are asking. Are you able to drink the cup that I drink, or be baptized with the baptism that I am baptized with?" They reply, "We are able" (Mark 10:39). Here is the best possible indication that James and John, who had been Jesus' companions for two years, just didn't get it. Jesus had just described for them that he was to be flogged, mocked, and crucified. They must have had no clue what he was talking about when he mentioned the cup that he would drink. Cocky, arrogant, self-absorbed—that's how I would describe their response. It is, I believe, what angered the other disciples; they were so sure that they were better than everyone else.

And I must say that this may be the message that today's church has preached to the sinners of this world more than any other. We're better than they are. We're God's chosen, they're not. We're holy, they're not. Of course, we don't actually say that. But we don't have to, because we're already living it. We're thinking it. We display it in our attitudes and actions. And no matter what we say about Jesus inside the church, it's what they see of Jesus in us outside the church that preaches better than any sermon I could ever deliver. And too often what folks are seeing in and hearing from those who have been hanging around Jesus on Sunday mornings is an arrogant, selfish, better-than-you attitude. Church of Jesus Christ, that is not our mission! It is not the mission of the church just to be blessed but to be a blessing. It is not the mission of the church to be better than others but rather to serve others. It is not the mission of the church to be more dignified than others. It is not the mission of the church to increase our self-esteem by acquiring prestige in the community. The mission of the church is to proclaim that Christ Jesus came to save sinners, of whom I—each and every one of us—am the foremost (1 Timothy 1:15). The mission of the church is to lift high the cross. The mission of the church is to go out into the highways and byways and compel people to come in so that God's house will be filled with God's children (Luke 14:23). The mission of the church is "Go therefore and make disciples of all nations" (Matthew 28:19). Whenever we allow our ego to exceed our reality, whenever we think more highly of ourselves than we do of others, whenever we forget who we were, where we came from, how messed up we were before Jesus saved us, before he delivered us, before he changed us, before he rearranged us—whenever we forget all this, then we just don't get it.

Jesus, the Undeterred Savior

I don't know about you, but I have to confess that on this score, I'm no better than James or John. I've been there and done that. I've allowed my personal ambition to run amok. I've allowed society's views of things to get in the way, even take over. I've allowed myself to think more highly of myself than I ought. There are times when I just don't get it. How about you? Have you been guilty of any or all of these things? And if so, is there a message for you and for me today? Is there any offering of hope for those of us who still don't get it today?

Well, I can only point out that in spite of the fact that James and John didn't get it, in spite of their personal ambition, their craving for societal acceptance, their high opinion of themselves in the face of a suffering servant, Jesus still decided to go to Jerusalem.

Knowing that many people just didn't get it, Jesus decided to go into the city riding on a donkey. Although they didn't understand a word of what Jesus was saying, he decided to let the chief priests and the scribes condemn him to death. They didn't get it, but he decided to let them flog him, mock him, crucify him. They didn't get it—we don't get it—but he decided to hang there on that cross for all.

We were looking for a grand and powerful leader, but he came as a humble and suffering servant. We were looking for glory, while he was offering humility. We were looking for personal fulfillment, while he was offering forgiveness of sins. We were looking for self-gratification, while he was offering himself as an atonement. We just didn't get it. We didn't understand him. We missed it so many times. We came to church and still didn't get it. We went to the "Hour of Power" and still didn't get it. We gave to the collection and still didn't get it. But thank God that while we were still lost in our trespasses and sins, Christ died for the ungodly. Thank God that he stayed on that cross for you and for me. Thank God that he cried out, "Father, forgive them; for they do not know what they are doing" (Luke 23:34).

You can imagine Jesus saying to his Father, "They just don't get it. They just don't understand. But there's a young man with a needle in his arm who needs me to die on this cross for his redemption. There's a young woman letting men abuse her and cheapen her body who needs to know that I love her and think the world of her. There's a Mexican in California who needs to be saved. There's a black woman downtown who needs a new life. There's a white man from the suburbs who needs a fresh start. There's a city full of people, a nation full of people, a world full of sinners who keep hating on each other, who keep warring with each other, who keep killing each other, and they need a savior for their souls. They need a redeemer. They need someone who can make all things new."

Is that you? Is that you today? Do you need a new life, a new start, a savior for your soul? Do you need to be forgiven for all the times you messed up? Are you humble enough to admit it—that it's not all about selfish ambition, that's it's not all about being politically correct, that it's not all about having a big ego, being filled with pride? Do you admit that you need Jesus today? Do you get it? If so, now is the time to tell him.

Cross Examinations

1. What are some of the things that you've been praying about lately, and what do those things reflect about you?
2. What does God want you to "get"?
3. In what ways have you put societal standards ahead of biblical mandates?
4. What is the mission of your church, and what is your role in that mission?

Note

1. *The Godfather: Part III,* directed by Francis Ford Coppola (Paramount, 1990).

It Can Happen to You
(Luke 22:1-6,21-23)

Then Satan entered into
Judas called Iscariot, who was
one of the twelve. (Luke 22:3)

Congratulations are in order. I got it in the mail just the other
day—an official envelope with a gold seal, saying that it could
happen to me: "You may have just won $10 million!" A movie,
based on a real-life incident involving a police officer and a cof-
fee-shop server who end up sharing a $4 million winning lottery
ticket, is titled *It Could Happen to You*.[1] And all my life I've been
taught to believe that good things can and will happen to me,
that miracles are real, that Jesus can and will do anything but
fail. There is nothing too hard for my God—no mountain too
high and no valley too low, no river too wide and no ocean too
deep. So no matter how bad the situation may look, no matter
how far off the victory, the blessing, the miracle that we need
may seem, I'm here to tell you that as long as you've got Jesus in
your life, it can happen to you.

Our biblical text contains a message involving the life of an
oft-reviled character named Judas Iscariot, whom Luke carefully
reminds us was one of the Twelve, chosen by Jesus. And our
theme is "It can happen to you." Before we pile criticism onto
Judas, deserved though it is, we need to get a picture of those individuals whom society has found it easy to condemn. Someone
gets convicted of a violent crime, and it's all over the news. And

people insist that a criminal like this should get the death penalty, as if they know this individual, as if they were there, as if they went to the trial and heard all the evidence. There is a tendency to want to kick someone when they're down without realizing that this individual is a real person. This person is someone's child, someone's spouse, someone's parent. And in many respects, we forget that very easily, given a simple turn of events one way or another, it may well have been us in that person's shoes.

"Judas called Iscariot." The derivation and the meaning of the name "Iscariot" are the subject of many discussions in theological circles. It is often assumed that it was his surname, like mine is "Flores." However, it may have been the name of his hometown. Another possibility is that the name came from Aramaic and meant "liar," so that he was essentially "the man of the lie." Another plausible theory is that "Iscariot" is derived from the Semitic form of the Latin word *sicarius*, meaning "dagger-bearer."[2] In Jesus' day many Jews were angry about the Roman occupation, frustrated and bitter because of their lack of freedom and respect. Some of these individuals were known as Zealots because their hatred for the Romans was so zealous that they would take any and every opportunity to exact revenge on Roman soldiers. A Zealot, spotting a Roman soldier walking along a street, would nonchalantly move in that direction, pull out a hidden dagger, and stab and kill the unwitting soldier before he even knew what hit him. Such Zealots would consider this act one small step toward the liberation of their homeland from Roman oppression.

These dagger-bearers held in their hearts the hope that one day God would provide a leader to overthrow the Roman government and return Israel to its autonomous state. Judas Iscariot was one of them, and he harbored in his heart the hope that Jesus was the man who would lead the Jews to military conquest over the Romans. Judas wasn't the only Zealot among the Twelve. One disciple was known as Simon the Zealot, and two others were called the Sons of Thunder. And then there were those who inquired immediately before Jesus' death and after his resurrection about when he would come into his kingdom, thinking that they would have cushy new government jobs in Jesus' new administration. "Judas called Iscariot," Luke records—the dagger-bearer, the Zealot, the one with hopes for restored autonomy and dignity for his people—"Satan entered into Judas called Iscariot."

The Devil Will Trip You Up

The devil is out there looking for a way to trip us up in God's plan for our lives. Luke tells us, "The chief priests and scribes were looking for a way to put Jesus to death" (Luke 22:2). Peter wrote about it this way: "Discipline yourselves, keep alert. Like a roaring lion your adversary the devil prowls around, looking for someone to devour" (1 Peter 5:8). I don't know how much you trust the Bible compared to what society is saying, but the Bible says that there is a real-life, no-fooling, out-to-get-you devil out there. And if you don't watch out, it can happen to you. If you're not careful, if you don't remain in Christ, if you don't stay prayed up, if you stray from the Lord, if you leave a door open for evil, the devil will tear you up. It can happen to you.

Look at Judas. Now, you may already have secured in your mind the image of villain for Judas. You may have vilified him and tossed him aside and thought disgusting thoughts about him, as he might well deserve. But watch out, because it could happen to you. "Judas called Iscariot," Luke says, was one of the Twelve. This was no drug pusher we're talking about. This was no player, no gang-banger, no thug. He wasn't all ghetto. He wasn't trippin'. He didn't have issues. No, Judas was one of the Twelve. It can happen to you.

It turns out that some of what the devil needs to mess up the lives of Christians is right in the church. Judas was noted to second-guess the wisdom of Jesus, and the devil can use that. Judas placed a high priority on money, and the devil can use that. Judas had some strong political leanings with which he became obsessed, so that when Jesus went in a direction contradictory to Judas's political party line and climbed a hill outside Jerusalem rather than a throne in Jerusalem, Judas had to make a choice as to what was more important to him: an insurrectionist or a savior, his party's politics or his Lord's teachings, his inclination for violence and military action to solve problems or the Lord's command to be peacemakers. The devil can take something as noble as Judas's quest to throw off Roman oppression and twist it into a betrayal of the Lord. And believe me, it can happen to you.

"Judas called Iscariot . . . was one of the twelve." The devil used Judas's obsession with his political ambitions. The devil used his love of money. The devil used his situation of being in poverty and tempted him with money and connections with people in powerful places. The devil was prowling around, looking for a way to trip him up, looking for a moment to deceive him, looking for a moment to ruin his life. Eventually, the devil got to him, Judas, one of the Twelve—perhaps a church member, a deacon, a trustee, a choir member, an usher, even a preacher. Believe me, it can happen to you.

The Devil Will Make You Give Up

Not only can the devil trip you up in various ways through various devices, but also he can make you give up. You know the story of how Judas, the treasurer of Jesus' congregation, received thirty pieces of silver for betraying the Lord. And then, after betraying Jesus, he committed suicide by hanging himself (Matthew 27:5). And if you know yourself to be in need of getting things right with the Lord before it's too late, but you still haven't brought yourself to take that step, don't think that the devil isn't plotting some way to get you to think about giving up on that idea. The devil is working overtime to convince people that God doesn't love them, that Jesus can't forgive them, that they've done something so horrible and selfish that God could never love them. Maybe you're a young person who has done something that you know is wrong and thought you'd never do. You were raised in the church, and you know right from wrong. You're in Jesus' circle, like Judas, one of the Twelve, was. And you find yourself contemplating giving up because you messed up, you blew it, you lost control, and you think that you've ruined your life.

That's how the devil works. He'll get you to hang around with the so-called in-crowd, to try a little of this and a little of that. And before you know it, you're so far from the Lord that you think that you can't ever get back. I'm telling you as a warning: it can happen to you. That's what the devil did to Judas. And that's what he wants to do to you. He wants you to give up on yourself, give up on your future, give up on your possibilities.

Jesus Came to Pick You Up

But something else, something radically different, can happen to you. Sure, the devil can trip you up and make you give up, but let me assure you of this: Jesus came to pick you up. Yes, Luke tells us that the devil entered into "Judas called Iscariot . . . who was one of the twelve." But Luke also reports that after the devil had tripped him up and messed him up and was making him give up, Jesus said, "See, the one who betrays me is with me, and his hand is on the table" (Luke 22:21). Now maybe we thought that Jesus died only for those disciples who didn't betray him. Maybe we thought that the table of the Lord was reserved for spotless saints who never messed up. Maybe we have it in our minds that Jesus saw Satan in Judas and threw him out the room. But the Bible says that after all that Judas had done, after Satan had tripped him up and messed him up, when it came time for Jesus to eat that final supper, to demonstrate his death by the bread and by the cup, Jesus made sure that Judas's hand was on the table.

Did you get that? Jesus broke that bread for Judas, sinner though he was. Jesus poured that wine into the cup for Judas, devil-infected though he was. Some of us tend to forget that Jesus came to seek and save those who are lost (Luke 19:10). We tend to forget that all we like sheep have gone astray (Isaiah 53:6), that there are none righteous, not even one (Romans 3:10), that all have sinned and come short of the glory of God (Romans 3:23). Yes, we tend to forget all that. And we tend to communicate to sinners that they don't deserve a place at the table of the Lord. But let me tell you, if Jesus had room at the table for Judas, then it can happen to you. No matter what you've done, Jesus died for you. No matter if you denied him, betrayed him, misunderstood him, turned your back on him, walked away from him, deserted him just as each and every one the Twelve did (Matthew 26:35,56), Jesus died on that cross for you, for your sins, for your shame, so that you could be forgiven, so that you could have a second chance, so that you could have a fresh start. His blood "reaches to the highest mountain and flows to the lowest valley; it will never lose its power."[3]

Maybe, in spite of all that, you're still thinking, "Not me. I'm just not good enough." But believe me, the Bible is filled with people who were not good enough, who blew it, who messed up. Noah got drunk (Genesis 9:21). Abraham and Sarah laughed at God (Genesis 17:17; 18:12). Jacob was a deceiver (Genesis 25:26).[4] Joseph had a prison record (Genesis 39:20). Moses was a murderer (Exodus 2:12). Rahab was a prostitute (Joshua 2:1). Samson was involved with a prostitute (Judges 16:1). David was an adulterer (2 Samuel 11:4). Jonah was stubborn and disobedient to God (Jonah 1:3). Peter denied Jesus three times (Matthew 26:75). Peter, James, and John fell asleep after Jesus asked them to stand watch (Matthew 26:43). Mary Magdalene was demon-possessed (Luke 8:2). Zacchaeus stole from poor people (Luke 19:8). Nevertheless, God loved each and every one of these individuals. And I assure you that no matter what you've done, Jesus can pick you up. It can happen to you. God still loves you. Jesus died for you.

I know that the devil may have tripped you up and messed you up. He may be even trying to get you to give up. But I'm reminding you that Jesus came to pick you up. Jesus came to clean you up. Jesus came to wash you up, dress you up, lift you up, and, as the psalmist says, he will lead you to a higher rock, a solid rock (Psalm 61:2). And one day, when the trumpet sounds, he's going to take you up (1 Corinthians 15:51). As the song says, "I'm goin' up yonder. I'm goin' up yonder to be with my Lord." And in the words of another song, "One of these ol' days . . . no more troubles." Someday, the foundations of the city where you live will be adorned with jewels, and the gates will be made of pearls, and the streets of pure gold (Revelation 21:19,21). It can happen to you. Don't give up. Don't let the devil mess you up. Don't let him trip you up. Instead, let Jesus pick you up.

Cross Examinations

1. In what ways do political alliances conflict with religious commitments?
2. How has money been an issue in your walk with Christ?

3. How has your church communicated God's forgiveness to sinners?

4. How did you respond to your biggest disappointment in life?

Notes

1. *It Could Happen to You,* directed by Andrew Bergman (Sony Pictures, 1994).

2. G. W. Buchanan, "Judas Iscariot," *International Standard Bible Encyclopedia,* vol. 2, ed. G. W. Bromiley (Grand Rapids: Eerdmans, 1982), 1151–53.

3. Andraé Crouch, "The Blood Will Never Lose Its Power," *The Blood* (Manna Music, Inc., 1966).

4. The name "Jacob" means "he grasps the heel," which is a Hebrew idiom meaning that someone is deceptive.

4

Witness for the Defense
(Matthew 26:57-68)

Now the chief priests and
the whole council were looking
for false testimony against
Jesus so that they might put
him to death. (Matthew 26:59)

There are several alarming aspects about the death of Jesus.
Among these is the fact that in this particular religious and legal
matter involving Jesus that went before Caiaphas the high priest
and later before Pilate the governor, Jesus had no witnesses for his
defense. Matthew says that the religious authorities were looking
for testimony from witnesses, but these were what we might
understand in our legal system today as witnesses for the prosecu-
tion, accusatory witnesses, witnesses who make the case that a
crime had been committed by the defendant.

False Testimony from False Witnesses

People were saying things about Jesus that simply were not true.
And the council, those bringing charges against Jesus, was seeking
out such untruth about Jesus and was ready to believe it and put
him to death for it. False witnesses were alleging things about Jesus
that never happened, accusing him of having been in places that he
never visited, maybe suggesting that he had a skeleton in his closet.
The same thing happens today: people make up things about Jesus.

A few years ago, some filmmakers created for popular con-
sumption the image of a Jesus who was filled with lust, who was

consumed with sexual immorality—false testimony from false witnesses. Some scholars see Jesus' resurrection as an unimportant and mythical aspect of his work of atonement, and they claim that he never did rise from the dead—false testimony from false witnesses.

Let me bring this a little closer to home for those who study their Bibles. There are false witnesses who will tell you their theory about religion and their interpretation of the Bible, which they've never read, never studied in depth, and for which they have absolutely no respect. They'll insist that no rational, thoughtful, well-educated, intellectually astute individual would adhere to this fairytale book. They'll state that Jesus was a nice person but certainly not the resurrected Savior, certainly not the Son of God, certainly not the coming King of Glory—false testimony from false witnesses.

There are those false witnesses who will say that they have lived all these many years and never needed Jesus, never needed a savior, never needed approval, love, and forgiveness from a benevolent and all-powerful God. "I'm okay on my own. I don't need a relationship with a universal creator. I don't need a relationship with a miracle-worker from Galilee, with a man who loves me so much that he would give his life for me. I'm fine just the way I am. I don't need to be born again. I don't need a new start. I don't need to go to church. I don't need to read the Bible. I don't need to pray, and I don't need anybody to pray for me." Have you heard somebody say anything along those lines? Have you known people who were lying to themselves when it comes to God, who were trying to convince you that they're just fine, when you know all along that they're lying? They're always complaining, always moaning, always whining, but they're telling you that they're happy just the way they are—false testimony from false witnesses.

Young people especially, watch out, because there are a whole lot of false witnesses out there trying to tell you false things about Jesus. They'll say that it isn't cool to try to do what Jesus said to do. They'll tell you that nobody follows *all* of Jesus' teachings. They'll tell you to be "like Mike" or that some hip-hop rapper is telling the truth, when actually it's Jesus who is "the way the truth and the life" (John 14:6). There are some false witnesses who will say that Christianity is old-fashioned, that it's not for today, that it's powerless, irrelevant, a waste of time—false testimony from false witnesses. Don't listen to those false witnesses. Don't give their false testimony any place in your heart. People who don't know Jesus cannot testify truthfully about someone they don't even know. If they've never met the man, if they've never listened to his teaching and his preaching, if they've never had a relationship with Jesus Christ, they can't possibly offer testimony that is worth anything at all.

The council was seeking false testimony from false witnesses about Jesus. The world today is seeking false testimony from false witnesses about Jesus. Don't be fooled. Don't let the lies and the deceit and the treachery of this world lead you to believe anything about Jesus that isn't true. False witnesses and false testimony abound today. A whole lot of folks are saying a whole lot of things about Jesus that just aren't so. Do you want to know about Jesus? Do you want to know who he is and why he came and what he did and what he said? Read the Bible for yourself. Read it. Don't trust other sources, people who haven't had a relationship with him, who don't know him, who don't know his love, faithfulness, forgiveness, grace, and mercy.

Dr. Jeremiah Wright tells the story of how, in the early 1970s, at the height of the "God is dead" theological movement, there was a conference in Chicago at the Moody Bible Institute. One of the world's leading theological scholars was brought in to give a seminar to the clergy of the city, updating them on the latest theological developments, sharing some of his new theories and latest writings. During the luncheon he went into his detailed and well-thought-out argument about how God was dead, how Jesus never rose from the dead, how there was mass hysteria or maybe mythical aspects added to his story years after his life concluded, including things such as walking on water, healing the sick, raising the dead, and rising from the grave. Then he took questions from the audience. One old preacher, who was finishing off his lunch, stood up, holding an apple in his hand. He said to the scholar, "I just have one question for you, what I perceive to be a very easy question to answer. This apple that I'm eating—is it bitter or sweet?" The scholar rolled his eyes and said, "Sir, obviously, since I've never tasted that apple, I can't know if it's bitter or sweet." And the preacher said, "And the same is true about Jesus. If you've never known him, you can't possibly know *about* him." Psalm 34:8 agrees, saying, "Taste and see that the LORD is good." And in his well-known hymn "I Serve a Risen Savior," Alfred Ackley declared, "You ask me how I know he lives? He lives within my heart."

Be careful what you hear out there—false testimony from false witnesses.

Witness for the Defense

One thing in particular strikes me about Jesus' trial: while the false witnesses were giving their false testimony against Jesus, no one rose to testify for his defense. The authorities asked him, "Have you no answer?" But Jesus was silent. There was no witness for the defense. I'm wondering what happened to the man born blind whose sight Jesus restored. Why wasn't he there to testify? Or what about the one grateful leper out of the ten that Jesus cleansed? What about Jairus, whose daughter Jesus healed? What about the Roman centurion whose deathly-ill servant Jesus cured from afar? Where was Lazarus, whom Jesus brought back from death? All of these people could have yielded pertinent and truthful testimony. Why was no one there to testify to Jesus' messiahship, to tell of the great things that he had done for them? Where were the witnesses for the defense?

Clearly, there were potential witnesses for Jesus' defense, but none stood up to testify on his behalf. There in the high priest's courtyard was Peter, following the whole affair from a safe distance (Matthew 26:58). He knew Jesus. However, there is a certain amount of political incorrectness when you're a witness for the defense. Then and now, an angry public wants to see people put to death. People want everybody who's charged with a crime to be convicted of a crime. There's a lynch-mob mentality that has pervaded our society for generations, and it hasn't gone away. So if you're going to testify for a defendant in this society, if you stand up for the accused, if you show solidarity with the sinner, then you yourself are guilty by association. And people know this.

One of the intriguing hearings before the trial of O. J. Simpson was when lawyers tried to compel football star Marcus Allen to come from Kansas City to California to testify for the defense. Marcus didn't want to go. He was a Heisman Trophy winner and MVP of the Super Bowl. He had a Hall of Fame career going. He had a future in broadcasting at stake. If he had testified for the defense, his financial future and employability would have been in jeopardy.

There is a certain amount of political incorrectness that attaches to anyone who is a witness for the defense. You're going to be attacked. You're going to be persecuted. Your character will be impugned. Every wrong thing that you ever did will be brought to light when you're a witness for the defense. People might threaten you if you testify for the defense. You'll never work again in this town if you testify for the defense. You'll be shunned by polite society. You'll be called names and be accused of being as villainous as the person for whom you're testifying. They'll question your sense of justice, your sense of fairness, and your compassion for the victim if you're a witness for the defense.

Peter was scared, and justifiably so. Try standing up for Christ today, and then watch what happens. See if people don't call you silly and superstitious. See if they don't call your mental faculties into question. See if they don't look down at you intellectually. See if they don't check out your past failures: "How can you be a Christian? I knew you when. You're talking about Jesus now, but I know how you used to be." No wonder people don't stand up for Jesus. No wonder people are afraid to mention his name, to call on him at work, to stand up for his word and ways, his ethics and love. You tell people that Jesus came to save them from their sins, and they'll tell you that nothing that they're doing is a sin. No, it's not easy being a witness for the defense. It's not easy standing up for Jesus. It's going to take something special to make you agree to be a witness for the defense. You're going to have to really believe if you're going to take all that. Jesus said that the world hated him, and so it will hate his disciples too, and that they would be reviled because of their allegiance to him (John 15:18; Matthew 5:11). No wonder Peter kept his distance. No wonder no one came to Jesus' defense.

What, then, makes for a good witness for the defense? Well, I watch a lot of *Law and Order* and *CSI*, so I've got my own law degree, sort of a video Juris Doctorate. First, a witness for the defense has to be available and willing to testify. Defense witnesses must be willing to endure the political and social fallout that might ensue. They must be courageous enough to come forward. They can't be cowardly, can't be a wimp, can't freak out and run when the going gets tough. They have to make themselves available to testify. Are you available to testify for Jesus? Are you willing to be reviled as he was reviled, to be shunned as he was, to have your good be spoken of as evil? Do you have the courage to be available to be a witness for the defense?

Second, a defense witness has to have some measure of credibility. If the witness is a drug addict, a felon, a racist, a thief, a liar—a "court-certified pathological liar," I once heard someone say—that will affect how people hear that person's testimony. How good is your credibility? Would anyone believe anything that you have to say about Jesus based on who you are and what you've done and what people see you doing? I'm not talking about salvation by works—thank God, we're saved by grace. But when you go to tell people about the Jesus who saved you, have you actually been saved from something, or are you still wallowing around in the same old sins? Are you changed and redeemed, or did you just go through some kind of revolving door and end up right back where you started? Do you have some measure of credibility when you testify that Jesus redeemed you, forgave you, gave you a new start?

Third, and perhaps most important, not only must a good witness be available and credible, but also a good witness must have personally seen or experienced something. In my *Law and Order* 101 class they taught us that certain kinds of testimony are inadmissible in a court of law. If you want to testify about something that you heard someone else talk about, that's hearsay, and it's inadmissible. If you want to testify about what you believe to have happened, even that is suspect because it's conjecture and speculation, and that too is inadmissible. In order to have a relevant testimony, in order to be an effective witness for the defense, in order to stand up for the defendant, you have to have seen or experienced something for yourself.

Do you have an experience with the risen Lord and Savior Jesus Christ? It can't be someone else's experience this time. Have you known Jesus for yourself? What do you think about Jesus? Not what your mother or father or your sister or brother says or knows, because that's all hearsay. That's all inadmissible. It's not enough that your preacher stood up for Jesus. It's not enough that your wife has a relationship with Jesus. That's all hearsay. It's not enough that you always thought about going to church. That's speculation, and it's inadmissible.

The question is, Do you personally know anything about Jesus? What do you think about Jesus? Have you been changed by his grace and his mercy? Did he ever heal you in the sick room? Did he ever defend you in the courtroom? Did he ever comfort you in the mortuary room? Did he ever love you when you were unlovely? Did he forgive you when no one else would? Did he give you a second chance when no one else would? Are you a witness for the defense today? If so, say so. Jesus can use you, and he will.

Cross Examinations

1. How is false testimony about Christ being offered today?
2. Discuss instances when you failed to stand up for Christ.
3. Discuss instances when you were a witness for Christ.
4. What things negatively affect your credibility as a witness for Christ, and how can you improve that?
5. What is your personal testimony concerning Christ?

Reality Faith
(Matthew 16:13-16; 26:69-74)

"You are the Messiah,
the Son of the living God."
(Matthew 16:16)

Then he began to curse,
and he swore an oath,
"I do not know the man!"
(Matthew 26:74)

Reality TV is programming that purports to show people as they really are. It is generally unscripted and undirected, oftentimes taking place in actual homes and workplaces, so that we can see how people really are and not just what a writer or producer wants to show us. Reality TV has so taken over the airwaves that on a recent summer evening, as I flipped through the channels looking for something entertaining with my family, I saw that all three major networks had some type of reality TV on. And since in many instances seeing people as they really are isn't so much entertaining for me as it is painful, I went to the video store and rented a Madea flick, and we had a great time with Tyler Perry.

Can we put a "reality TV" camera on Peter? In which of these two Scripture texts do we see Peter as he really is? These two verses force us to face one of life's most difficult tasks: understanding who we really are. Are we saints who have clothed ourselves with the holiness of Christ, or are we sinners whose soiled robes need a thorough washing in Christ's blood? Are we conscientious and concerned Christians who are serving others, or are we uncommitted and uncaring individualists who can't be bothered with anyone else? Which is the real you, the real me? Two quick glimpses at Peter in the Gospel of Matthew reveal a follower of Jesus who at one point declares his belief that Jesus is the Christ but then, just a few chapters later, denies that he even knows who Jesus is. Have you and I been there and done that too?

Sunday Christians

When I was a teenager in my father's church, we often used the term *dominguero,* "Sunday Christian." It referred to those who went to church only on Sundays but never came to Bible study or prayer meeting, never got involved in a church program or mission project, never helped out by teaching the youth. Sometimes I would bump into these folks outside the church community—kind of like the way we bump into Peter at the end of Matthew 26—and I discovered, much to my naïve surprise, that some people behave one way in church and a totally different way in the high priest's courtyard. My cousin would say, "Hey, doesn't he go to your church?" And I'd reply, "Yeah, but he's a *dominguero.*" Oh, okay, got it.

And maybe that's been the problem with the church in general for these many centuries, and maybe that's why so many are turned off by the church these days. People see Christians, who claim to have faith, and notice that they look like one thing on Sundays but like something quite different the rest of the week. On Sundays we worship the Prince of Peace, but on Mondays we're fighting with our neighbors. On Sundays we're giving to the church to expand the building, but on Mondays we're grumbling about our taxes that support programs for the poor. On Sundays we're sober and upright, but on Mondays we're drunk and disorderly. On Sundays we're in a church pew seated next to our family, but on Mondays we're in a motel bed with someone who isn't our spouse. On Sundays we break bread and take the cup together, but on Mondays we're breaking the law and taking advantage of others. You almost want to ask, like in that old TV game show, "Will the real church please stand up?"

For centuries there has been this gap in the Christian church between precept and practice, between what we say we believe and what we actually live out, between the sweet love of a redemptive Jesus and the bitter reality of war and poverty around the world. I can remember in college studying European history from the Middle Ages until the modern era and noting how horrendously at times the church has behaved toward Muslims, Jews, Native Americans, black Africans, and others. The absurdity of the Crusaders having a cross emblematic of the suffering of Jesus on their uniforms and helmets as they pillaged and plundered and inflicted atrocities on innocent human beings is the epitome of scandal. And this brand of duplicitous Christianity may well have roots in biblical history—case in point, the two different Peters who appear in Matthew 16 and Matthew 26, giving two entirely different responses to a question about Jesus.

I've always been amazed at how utterly human and real the characters in the Bible are, especially when we look at their stories through the lenses of our own fallibility. Peter, we like to think, was weak. Peter was a failure. Peter was a fool. Peter denied the Lord. We'll look down our noses with utter condescension at a person like that and think to ourselves, as we read the text from our cushioned pews in comfortable churches, "How terrible for someone to do that to our Lord." Terrible indeed. And how much more terrible to have read the story and repeated the folly!

I'm an avid golfer—not necessarily a good one, but an avid one. If you know anything about that sport, you know that it has the ability to make even the saintliest person blow a fuse. It can frustrate you to no end trying to hit that little white ball. It is the most difficult sport I've ever played, and I've played many of them. I golf with several preacher friends of mine, one of whom was with me on a very frustrating day on the course. When I totally misplayed one shot, I looked to the heavens and shouted, "Aaaggghh!" After a long pause, my friend said, "That's it? Every other red-blooded American would be cursing a blue streak." Matthew tells us that Peter cursed. He lost his cool and started cursing like a sailor. And my friend that day on the golf course told me, "You never curse. You're the real deal. That's why I admire you."

And as we played our round of golf that day, I told my friend what happened to me once when I was a kid in elementary school.

We had just had one of those open-house days when you bring your family to the school, and mom and dad get to see what you've been doing with their tax dollars. But it also was an opportunity for the kids to see the parents. And my dad, bless his heart, was always on the clock. Every other dad that evening was dressed casually, in jeans and a sweater or something like that. But not my dad, the Rev. Aureliano Flores. He was dressed in his suit and tie, looking every bit the preacher. And everyone knew that my dad was a pastor. "That's why you never curse," some of them said to me. "No wonder you're such a goody-goody." And the next day in school someone got in my face, and we started hollering at each other. The argument kept heating up, and finally I lost it and let out one loud curse word—loud enough that the whole playground heard it. And then it started: "Wow, the church kid, the preacher's son. Some Christian you are. Now we know the real Ernie." Even the kid I was yelling at was laughing so hard at me that he forgot what we were arguing about. I was so ashamed.

So who was "the real Ernie"? And who is the real Christian? And what is the real church? Are we a bunch of hypocrites and liars? Are we capable of proclaiming our faith in Christ only in a setting where others believe the same thing? Are we somehow like Peter? Are we saints who sing hymns of praise to Jesus on Sundays but who, at the first opportunity to bear witness to people who don't believe in him, deny him, thus following them away from him rather than leading them toward him? Who are we really?

Remembering What Jesus Says

Matthew tells us, "Then Peter remembered what Jesus had said: 'Before the cock crows, you will deny me three times.' And he went out and wept bitterly" (Matthew 26:75). Maybe this is the real test of our faith and devotion to Christ. Peter, when he let down the Lord, when he blew it in front of a world that was hating Jesus, "wept bitterly." Matthew clearly is trying to communicate how deep was the pain that Peter felt when he let the Lord down.

Now, it goes without saying that all of us have let the Lord down. But have we ever wept over it? Have we felt the sting of self-disappointment and shame from having injured the one who loves us the most? Because that might well be the deal-breaker for the world in trying to make sense of our claim to faith in Jesus Christ: Do we care when we make mistakes? Does it hurt us to know that we may have hurt others? Are we humble enough to admit that we're not perfect, that we make mistakes, that we mess up from time to time? Does our awareness of our humanity lead us to a humility that produces sincerity and meekness and an understanding heart toward those who, just like us, are far from perfect? Or do we instead attempt to cover up our imperfections, pretend that we've never made any mistakes, and allow that to produce in us an arrogance, pretentiousness, and conceit that no sinner would ever open up to?

I think that it's high time that we regain the reality of our faith, the crux of the gospel, that we resist the temptation to focus our religion on ourselves and our own accomplishments and instead reinstate Jesus as the center of our faith. For the reality of our faith is not that we are good, not that we are perfect, not that we are without blemish, but rather that Christ Jesus came to save sinners, of whom I—each and every one of us—am the foremost (1 Timothy 1:15). The reality of our faith, as James Rowe put it in "Love Lifted Me," is this:

> I was sinking deep in sin,
> Far from the peaceful shore.
> Very deeply stained within,
> Sinking to rise no more.
> But the Master of the sea,
> Heard my despairing cry,
> From the waters lifted me,
> Now safe am I.

And I'm so glad about that—not in a manner that makes me forget my sinfulness or that catapults me into some status of the pristine and the perfect, but in such a way that expresses my deep appreciation for the grace of God bestowed upon me. He didn't have to love me. I don't deserve his faithfulness. I was lost in my trespasses and sins when Jesus died for the ungodly.

The Scripture says, "Then Peter remembered what Jesus had said" (Matthew 26:75). I believe that this is a habit that all Christians ought to have embedded into our code of conduct: whenever we blow it, whenever we let Jesus down, not only should we weep bitterly and feel the sting of our shame, but also we should remember *all* of what Jesus says. Besides predicting our failures, as he did with Peter, Jesus says, "Anyone who comes to me I will never drive away" (John 6:37). Jesus says, "Come to me, all you that are weary and are carrying heavy burdens, and I will give you rest" (Matthew 11:28). Jesus says, "There will be more joy in heaven over one sinner who repents than over ninety-nine righteous persons who need no repentance" (Luke 15:7). Jesus says, "God did not send the Son into the world to condemn the world, but in order that the world might be saved through him" (John 3:17). Jesus says, "Neither do I condemn you. Go your way, and from now on do not sin again" (John 8:11). Please, remember what Jesus says.

Cross Examinations

1. If a hidden camera had been focused on you during the past three days, what would an objective observer determine about the real you?
2. What are you doing in ministry at your church? With the youth? For missions? For community outreach and social justice?
3. How do you respond to charges from non-Christians about the sins of the historical church?
4. What is the focus of the gospel message that you share with others? Why?

6

A Slap in the Face
(Matthew 26:57-68)

They spat in his face and
struck him; and some slapped
him. (Matthew 26:67)

On March 27, 2005, the membership of the church that I pastor marched into its newly renovated facility for Easter Sunday worship services. With all the dreams and excitement and inspiration that went into the building renovation and those worship services, I'm not so sure that I properly guided my congregation toward the cross of Calvary in the season of Lent before that Easter Sunday. It's a mistake, perhaps even an insult, to the sacrificial work of Jesus, the spotless Lamb of God, not to focus sufficient attention on the horrific suffering that he underwent in order to catch our falling souls. It's easy and desirable to focus our daily thoughts on the goodness of God, on how blessed we are, on how bright our pathway is. But to do so without so much as a pause—a healthy, contemplative pause—to ponder how it is that we came to be so blessed is a disservice to our Lord, even a slap in the face. So let's return to those bitter moments of history when a young man who had done no wrong went on trial for his life.

Cruel and Unusual Punishment

It was common during the biblical era for prisoners to suffer indignities inflicted upon them by their captors, or by prison guards, or even by bystanders. There was never any public outcry against the inhumane treatment of prisoners; there was no Geneva Convention or U.S. Constitution to protect against cruel and unusual punishment in those days. Filled with contempt or hatred or vengeance for prisoners, people would mock them, as some Roman soldiers did to Jesus (Matthew 27:29), or spit on them, as Matthew notes in our text (see also Matthew 27:30). And beating and slapping were also among the indignities permitted and accepted in that era. Our own modern saying "That's a slap in the face" originates from such humiliation, an insulting act that contradicts human dignity.

The Scripture declares that Caiaphas the high priest was so enraged at hearing Jesus declare himself to be the Son of God, at his articulation of how he would soon be seated at the right hand of God, that he lost his temper, ripped his clothes, proclaimed that Jesus had committed blasphemy, and demanded a verdict from the equally appalled gathering of scribes and elders. When they perceived Jesus to be blaspheming, it was all they could do to refrain from killing him right there and then. But at the very least they already knew that this condemned man was to be the target of indignities that they would inflict. They spat in his face. They struck him. And some slapped him. Such reprehensible conduct aimed at our Lord, degrading him, humiliating him, intentionally dishonoring him, deserves our consideration if for no other reason than that we might come to understand the mindset of those who engaged in such behavior toward him.

The high priest Caiaphas and the scribes and elders were filled with envy and jealousy toward Jesus. So angered were they at the sound of what they perceived to be his blasphemy that they would do anything to show their resentment of him, their repudiation of his claim to be God's Son. Not only did their spitting dishonor the Lord, but also it was beneath their own human dignity. Spitting on prisoners may have been a societal norm at that time, but in any era it would make any person cringe to spit on someone else intentionally. Yet because they resented Jesus with such a passion, because they disagreed so vehemently with what he was saying, because they were intent on rejecting his claim to be God's Son, they engaged in the hideous conduct of spitting on a fellow human being. They degraded themselves in an attempt to display their resentment for our Lord.

Is It I, Lord?

There are those today who still engage in such behavior, who purpose in their heart that no Jesus and no Bible is ever going to tell them what to do. They are so angered that a religion or a religious figure or a God would have the audacity to tell them what to do that they react with rebellious and resentful conduct that actually shames them more than anyone else. We think of some rebellious teenagers who stick needles in their arms, or who abuse their bodies, or who hang out with individuals who have no sense of shame, no regard for their own dignity or humanity. Many times such behavior by young people reflects the desire to inflict injury on parents or on authority figures by self-abuse and self-abasement. Sometimes we injure ourselves in order to inflict emotional injury on others.

"They spat in his face and struck him; and some slapped him." Sometimes it is not necessarily self-destructive conduct, but any conduct intended to run directly contrary to the desires of the authority figure. Nobody likes to be struck or slapped, and yet that is exactly what these religious leaders did, because they could, because they desired to show their defiant attitude toward Jesus' claim to be the Son of God. We must not forget that these people were the religious leaders of that day, and that they believed in the rightness of their assessment of Jesus' credentials. And to show their disdain for this would-be messiah, they spat on him and struck him, and some slapped him. They gave him the exact opposite treatment from what the Son of God deserved. They rebelled directly against his claim to be God's Son.

I wonder how many cases there are today involving people doing exactly the opposite of what God desires simply to cause injury to our Lord. It is the nature and essence of sin to rebel against what God requires of us. Just as it was with Adam and Eve, who were persuaded by a cunning serpent that God didn't really mean what he said, so it is with many of God's children today: they are convinced that God didn't really mean "You shall not murder" (Exodus 20:13), that Jesus didn't really mean it when he said, "Turn the other cheek" (Matthew 5:39), and that he must have been misunderstood when he said, "Love your enemies and pray for those who persecute you" (Matthew 5:44). No wonder our country continues to go to war with anyone who threatens us. No wonder our society is saturated with images of sexual promiscuity. No wonder illegal drugs are a billion-dollar-a-year industry. No wonder kids are dying of overdoses and gun violence daily. Apparently, many people don't believe that Jesus actually meant what he said, for they are doing exactly the opposite of what Jesus requires of us. And just as it was when the high priest and the scribes and elders did it to our Lord, so it is today: a slap in the face—an act of resentment, a display of rebellion toward him.

Actually, in Matthew 26–27 there's no shortage of individuals who were slapping Jesus in the face, even though, unlike those in the house of Caiaphas the high priest, they weren't physically striking him. But imagine what it must have felt like for Jesus to be serving supper to his disciples, to be washing their feet and describing his death for them, only to have one of them plotting to betray him all the while. Wasn't that a slap in the Lord's face? Wasn't that an indignity toward Jesus and a total devaluation of all that he was doing? And before we get too judgmental about this betrayer, Judas Iscariot, we should note that probably there are some folks who come to church and hear about Jesus' love and sacrifice and grace and mercy, and all the while they're devising some plan to sin against him—while they're in church! Perhaps they've got designs on someone else's spouse, or they're planning to pass on some juicy bit of gossip about a deacon or the pastor, or they're figuring out a way to rob God by not giving their tithe. Color it up any way you want, but those are acts of betrayal. God looks at the heart. God knows what we're doing. God is watching you and me. God knows what's on our minds and in our hearts. Even while we sit in the church, even while we take the bread and the cup, even while we sing God's praise, if we're plotting, like Judas, to injure our Lord by betraying him, then we are slapping him in the face.

How often do we do this? We sit in church on a Sunday morning singing "Love Lifted Me," and on Monday morning we fume with hatred toward our boss at work. During worship the Scripture is read, "Do not judge, so that you may not be judged," and we're looking at someone in the next pew and thinking, "How on earth could she wear that blouse with that skirt?" The preacher proclaims how Jesus told us to love our neighbor, and we're thinking, "Jesus never would have said that if he had lived next to *my* neighbor." This might be humorous if it weren't so tragic, that we could, with such hypocrisy, with such disregard for the desires of our Lord, with such little respect for how we're injuring him every time we do it, be in the presence of God and be slapping our Savior in the face by our acts of betrayal.

This is getting uncomfortable, but I believe that when we consider what Jesus endured for us all, and endures for you and for me, we should not feel at ease. "They spat in his face and struck him; and some slapped him." Surely we are above such conduct. Surely we are better than those who resented Christ and desired nothing more than to display their resentment and rebelliousness toward him. Surely we are not like that. And of the Twelve, Judas Iscariot was the one person who so betrayed the Lord, who plotted against Jesus even while Jesus was going to the cross for him. Surely we are not so deceptive and malicious. Are we?

Broken Promises, Forgiving Savior

There is another person whose behavior toward Jesus, though predicted by our Lord, was no less harmful and injurious to him. For there in the courtyard outside the home of Caiphas the high priest sat Peter, one of the best-known disciples, a man whose very name is synonymous with the church. Peter was so well intentioned that when Jesus discussed his plans to go to Jerusalem to be killed, Peter tried to protect his Lord by stopping him from going (Matthew 16:21-22). He declared to the Lord, "Though all become deserters because of you, I will never desert you" (Matthew 26:33). But less than twelve hours later, there was Peter in the courtyard, doing the very thing he denied he would do. A servant-girl said to him, "You also were with Jesus the Galilean."

Another servant-girl said to some bystanders, "This man was with Jesus of Nazareth." And finally a few bystanders confronted him and said, "Certainly you are also one of them, for your accent betrays you." And each time, Peter denied that he knew the Lord (Matthew 26:69-74). And that last time, he degraded himself by cursing and swearing an oath, exactly contrary to what Jesus had taught, and contrary even to Peter's own expectations for himself.

Have you ever let down the Lord? Have you made a promise and not kept it? And I'm not some prosecutor looking to inflict emotional harm on you while eliciting condemning testimony. I too am one of those who are convicted by this very passage, of letting God down, of letting myself down. Despite our best efforts, despite our aim to be pleasing in the Lord's sight, despite our knowledge of God's word or what is right or wrong, we still find ourselves, like Peter, sitting in that courtyard, breaking our Lord's heart. Haven't you done that? You didn't plan on it. It wasn't your intention to do it. It was the farthest thing from your mind. But there it is. You denied him. You failed him. You broke his heart and yours. You slapped him in the face.

There may be no more severe injuries than those inflicted by a friend. And how often we have most injured and slapped around our own Lord and Savior, Jesus Christ—with our betrayal, with our rebellion, with our failure to do what we said we should do.

And here is the amazing thing about this whole story. Although the scribes and the elders spat on him and struck him and slapped him, although Judas plotted against him and betrayed him, and although Peter failed him and broke his heart, Jesus decided to die anyway. "While we were still weak, Christ died for the ungodly. . . . While we were still sinners Christ died for us" (Romans 5:6,8). His death was for us, who were lost in our trespasses and sins, who like sheep had gone astray, who had rebelled and spurned and intentionally injured him. We are the ones he died for. We are the reason that, as the old spiritual says, "He never said a mumblin' word." We are the reason he endured the shame and indignity of the cross. We are the reason.

I'm so glad that he looked beyond my faults and saw my needs. I'm so glad that he didn't render unto me according to my works.

I'm so glad that he put my sins as far from him as east is from west. "Though your sins are like scarlet, they shall be like snow; though they are red like crimson, they shall become like wool" (Isaiah 1:18). Even though we've given him a slap in the face, he's given us forgiveness of our sin.

Cross Examinations

1. What causes people to neglect the suffering of Jesus?
2. In what ways do people today slap Jesus in the face?
3. In what ways in your life have you slapped Jesus in the face?
4. How has the grace of Jesus affected your life?

7

The Slippery Slope of Betrayal
(Matthew 27:1-10)

> When Judas, his betrayer, saw that Jesus was condemned, he repented and brought back the thirty pieces of silver to the chief priests and the elders.
>
> (Matthew 27:3)

There are those moments when we have gone too far, when we have done worse than we ever expected, when we have betrayed ourselves, our families, our God, when in our lostness we just wish that we could take it back. Monday-morning quarterbacks excel at second-guessing the decisions of football coaches and players, but they have the luxury of doing so without the pressures and consequences of having to make real decisions in the actual game. It's the real-life quarterback who would love to have a second chance, a chance to take back the intercepted pass or change the call to a game-winning play. Athletes who had a chance and blew it, who sealed their fates with performances that were less than their best—they are the ones who must bear the pain and shame of their failures.

Perhaps such athletes embody a lesson from Matthew 27, where Judas the betrayer repented of his sins. He had obtained thirty pieces of silver in exchange for selling out his Savior. But in the aftermath of his abominable behavior, stung by the realization of his iniquities, Judas understood what horrific wrong he had performed, and he sought to turn back the clock. He tried to awaken from the nightmare of his own creation, to be free from the burden of his self-imposed calamity, and to make things the way they were before he committed his catastrophic act of betrayal.

Have you ever felt like that? Have you ever done something so foolish, so sinful, so contrary to what you believe yourself to be that with all your heart, mind, soul, and strength you wanted to erase certain moments in history and make them as though you had done no wrong? Betrayal was what Judas had performed to perfection, and it was betrayal from which he, unsuccessfully, yearned to be free. He repented, Matthew tells us, and brought back the thirty pieces of silver. Perhaps Judas had come to his senses, like the young man in Jesus' parable who, after sinking to unforeseen depths of sin and shame in betraying his father, "came to himself" (Luke 15:17). Maybe, after seeing the fate of crucifixion that had come to Jesus, after pondering afresh exactly what it was he had been party to, what he had initiated and was responsible for, maybe when all that came crashing down upon his soul, Judas came to himself.

If the Name Fits . . .

I've often wanted to be a fly on the wall when great events were taking place, when marvelous plans were taking shape, when an important leader was contemplating decisions of war and peace, when a genius poet was penning a sonnet or a master composer was creating a symphony. But I think that more valuable would be to have had access to the machinations of the heart and mind of Judas at this moment described in the Scriptures. All of us would profit from an understanding of the inner workings of this infamous figure. For in this man we have an individual whose betrayal of Christ so shamed him that no parent now would even think of naming a child after him. There are Samuels, Davids, Peters, and Pauls in abundance. Every classroom roster will contain plenty of biblical names, but not a single "Judas" will be found.

In biblical times, however, "Judas" was one of the more popular names. About 150 years before Christ, Judas Maccabeus led a great revolt that saw the Jewish people win their freedom and autonomy for what would be the last time for some two thousand years. Every mother loved that name. Every father was proud to give that name. Every Judas was honored to bear that name. But the actions of Judas Iscariot were of such magnitude that even the greatness of Judas Maccabeus was overshadowed, and the name "Judas" became emblematic of depravity and betrayal that only the vilest of sinners could attain: "That person's a Judas." That name provokes an angry response and denial from anyone tagged with it, doesn't it? No one wants to be called "a Judas."

And yet, each and every one of us, sometime in our lives, must admit that the name fits us—if we are honest, anyway. Paul was honest about it, acknowledging that he was the foremost among sinners (1 Timothy 1:15). "All have sinned," he said, "and fall short of the glory of God" (Romans 3:23). If we are honest, we will confront ourselves and realize our betrayal of God, of our calling, of our own selves. And our text from Matthew's Gospel contains a warning that such acts of betrayal do not occur suddenly, and that we may well be engaged in the process of descending this slippery slope of betrayal right now and not even know it. It is not as though sin overtakes us in a moment, in the twinkling of an eye. For Judas and for us as well, it is a slippery slope that gradually and efficiently separates us from our Savior and from our best efforts. No one simply wakes up one day and decides, "I'm going to betray God today."

The racism and fascism of Nazi Germany in the first half of the twentieth century did not appear out of thin air; they resulted from the accumulation of hatred over centuries that led to the horrors of genocide. It didn't just happen; there was a process. And in our own country, the two major political parties have a long way to go in terms of social justice. Why is it that the Republican Party, the party of Abraham Lincoln and Frederick Douglass, a party rooted in the movement to abolish slavery, captures less than 15 percent of black voters in national elections? It wasn't an overnight process. History shows that it was a slippery slope: the outrageous actions of greedy carpetbaggers, then acquiescence to Jim Crow laws, then the presidency of a Democrat whose New Deal policies provided jobs for many of the nation's poor and minorities, then the dirty politics of winning the votes of the legion of white Southern Democrats during the Civil Rights Movement, then a general opposition to affirmative action, and the party of Lincoln and Douglass had lost the support of the vast majority of the black community. But on the other hand, unlike the current Republican president, no Democratic president has ever appointed a black secretary of state or a Hispanic attorney general. Perhaps there is a slippery slope ahead for the Democrats as well.

But the betrayal of minorities by political parties, important as that topic is, is not our focus for this text. What I want us to contemplate here is how we Christians betray our Christ, and how we betray Christ's gospel and our mission as the church. How is it that many Baptist churches never baptize anyone? How is it that many preachers of the gospel use their pulpit as a platform for supporting political candidates instead of as a foundation for calling sinners to repentance and proclaiming Christ's power to save them? Most importantly, Christians most of all must be aware that it is a slippery slope that leads to betrayal. It rarely happens suddenly; most often it happens gradually, slowly and surely. And before you know it, you wake up to yourself, like Judas did, and you realize how far you've strayed from your goal. You wake up and see how far away from God you've slid. You wake up and see how shameful you've become, even though you had no idea that what you were doing was leading you further and further astray from the way of our Savior.

Signs on the Slope

How was it that Judas descended this slippery slope of betrayal? What was the process in which he engaged, and how might we be better aware of and forewarned about this slippery slope? Let's look at some Scriptures that depict Judas heading down this slope ever so gradually. In John 12:5, after a woman has anointed Jesus with a costly perfume, Judas said, "Why was this perfume not sold for three hundred denarii and the money given to the poor?" A noble thought, we might believe. But the Gospel writer comments, "He said this not because he cared about the poor, but because he was a thief; he kept the common purse and used to steal what was put into it" (John 12:6). Be warned, Christians, that when your actions are motivated by greed instead of grace, you're descending the slippery slope of betrayal. No wonder the Ten Commandments forbid covetousness (Exodus 20:17), and Paul condemns greed as idolatry (Colossians 3:5). Look at the economic sins of this world, and see greed driving them. Look at the wars around the world, and see greed for land, power, and wealth lurking behind them. Judas was greedy.

John 12:6 also reveals that Judas practiced deception. On one level, he told the truth: the money could indeed have been used to help the poor. But he was being deceptive, because that had nothing to do with his real motivation for suggesting that the perfume be sold. And what about you and me? If we have to make up stories to account for our whereabouts, when we no longer can lay bare our soul for fear of the revelation of deceptions that lie therein, then we are descending the slippery slope of betrayal. If you can't tell your spouse where you were last night and have to hide your e-mails, if you can't tell Uncle Sam the truth about how you made or spent your money, if you can't even tell the whole truth to your pastor or other Christians to whom you are accountable, then you may well be descending the slippery slope of betrayal.

Matthew 26:15 reports other words from Judas that reveal even more about this slippery slope of betrayal. In the process of negotiation with the chief priests, Judas said, "What will you give me if I betray him to you?" I shudder every time I read those words—not only for their expressions of greed and deception, but also for the selfishness on display. Surely we can see that when we have moved into the arena of putting ourselves first, of seeking our own above all others, of neglecting God and others to act in sheer self-interest, we are far down the slippery slope of betrayal. What will you give me? What's in it for me? Taking care of "number one" is a sure sign that we are in trouble and in danger of having drifted away from the shoreline of God's love. All of the law and the prophets insist that we love God and others. Jesus himself said it to us (Matthew 22:37-39).

So, when we allow greed to drive us, and then practice deception and concealment of our real self, and then give selfishness free rein, it adds up to deterring us from being a friend to anyone but ourselves. At that point, we must be awakened, like Judas, to what we are doing. We are betraying our God. We are sinning against the Lord. We are leaving our roots. We are forsaking the very one who created us and loved us, who died for us and sought to redeem us. This is how we end up so far away from our Lord. This is how we do things that we never thought we would do. This is how we break God's heart and ruin our lives. It all starts when, ever so unnoticeably, we begin to travel down that slippery slope of betrayal.

The Right Place to Repent

There are consequences to our actions of betrayal. Some have focused on the life of Judas as an illustration—his defection, his disgrace, his suicide. But reading Matthew 27:1-10, and noting that powerful statement "He repented," I am deeply disturbed to think that Judas's repentance was not good enough. I could tell you that repentance will not bring back the person whom you've killed nor even restore the spouse whom you've alienated. I could tell you that, but as a gospel preacher it is the bedrock of my goal that I see sinners come to repentance. And here is the story of a man who repented but still goes down in history as a traitor, a liar, a thief. This disciple from Jesus' own inner circle, this "churchgoing" man, repented, but still he was scarred with pain and misery over his misconduct and betrayal of his Savior. And his guilt and shame so overwhelmed him that he could see no other recourse but to kill himself.

But notice something crucial about Judas's repentance: he went to the chief priests and the elders to repent—his co-conspirators, those whose own selfishness, greed, and deception helped bring about the crucifixion of Jesus. And it may be the most deadly effect of this slippery slope of betrayal that Judas lost his sense of direction. For he went to the chief priests and elders to repent, and they said to him, "What is that to us?" (Matthew 27:4). In other words, "Too bad. You're on your own." Judas found no solace there. He turned to human institutions and found no rest for his weary soul there. He turned to the powers that be, and they were powerless to offer him any peace.

So, I can't help but wonder how the story would have turned out if the betrayer had repented to Jesus instead. What would have happened if Judas had gone to him who said, "Anyone who comes to me I will never drive away" (John 6:37)? What would have happened if he had gone to the one who had preached, "Repent, and believe in the good news" (Mark 1:15)? How would Judas's epitaph have read had he turned to a loving and merciful Savior instead of to a cold and cruel system? What would Judas have become if in his pursuit of absolution he had gone to the throne of mercy instead of to the courts of law? What would Judas have become had he known "All we like sheep have gone astray . . . and the LORD has laid on him the iniquity of us all" (Isaiah 53:6)? How would Judas's story have ended?

Come to think of it, I do know the end of that story. I *am* the end of that story. I once was lost in sins, but Jesus set me free. I betrayed him time and time again, but in his steadfast love he died for me while I was yet a sinner. He took upon himself my sins, my sorrows, my penalty, my punishment. I know what would have happened to Judas because I *am* what would have happened to Judas. I've descended that slippery slope of betrayal. I know what it's like to let God down and break God's heart. I know what it's like to feel trapped in your sins, wishing that you could take it back, hoping that it's all just a nightmare and you can wake up and not be the sinful betrayer that you've become. I've been there.

But when I repented, I came to *Jesus,* no one else. And that has made all the difference. He did not refuse me. He did not reject me. He did not cast me out. He did not condemn me, even though I surely deserved it. He put his arms around me; he took me in and didn't throw me out. He loved me and didn't hate me. He said, as Tupac Shakur put it, "I ain't mad at ya. Ain't got nothing but love for ya." I said, "But Lord, I've messed up, I betrayed you, I was selfish, I was foolish." And he said, "I'm not mad at you. I've got nothing but love for you."

"But Lord," someone will say, "I ruined my marriage, I abandoned my children, I got myself hooked on drugs."

"I'm not mad at you," Jesus answers. "I've got nothing but love for you."

"But I'm so ashamed of myself, so appalled at how low I've sunk."

"I'm not mad at you. I've got nothing but love for you."

Even if you've slid to the very bottom of the slippery slope, repent to Jesus, and then listen carefully for that voice: "I'm not mad at you. I've got nothing but love for you."

Cross Examinations

1. Can you think of examples of when you have somehow betrayed Christ?
2. Is it possible to get rid of a bad reputation? If so, how?
3. How have you attempted to make up for wrong things that you've done?
4. When you have done something wrong, do you have a hard time accepting Christ's forgiveness? If so, why?

8

The Pilate Perspective
(Luke 23:1-5,13-25)

He handed Jesus over as
they wished. (Luke 23:25)

It happens all too often these days: people who come to know Christ sell him out to a world insistent on the demise of its loving Savior. Our great Savior, who loves us and gave himself for us, is in our hearts, seeking for us to love him back with the passion and service that he himself displayed for us. And yet too often what we do instead is take the path that Pilate took: "He handed Jesus over as they wished." We do what everyone wants us to do or whatever will make us more accepted and more liked by our friends and by those whom we esteem, and we surrender our commitment to the one who loved us with every last drop of his blood and every ounce of love in his being. What a sad episode played out in the early morning hours when our Lord Jesus was condemned by the religious establishment, and when the legal process took him on a failed pursuit of justice before the man called Pontius Pilate.

What to Do with Jesus

Pilate's perspective on and interaction with Jesus are not all that unfamiliar if we take a closer look at him and perform a thorough examination of ourselves. The trouble throughout Luke 23 centers on Pilate having a decision to make about what to do with Jesus. People came to Pilate and told him that he should condemn Jesus to death, and Pilate had to decide what to do with Jesus. We

53

have a similar problem in our lives on a daily basis: what to do with Jesus. Shall we begin the day with a word of prayer, or shall we instead turn on CNN or Fox News and allow the media to start our day for us?

What to do with Jesus. Do we dress in a way that honors and celebrates the body that God gave us or in a way that flaunts sexuality and signals promiscuity? Do we treat women with the dignity and respect due a child of God created in the image of God, or do we regard them as sexual playthings and punching bags? Do we remain silent and thus give tacit support to preemptive warfare waged by our government against anyone perceived to be our enemy, or do we follow Jesus, who taught us to love our enemies, turn the other cheek, and forgive others so that our heavenly Father may also forgive us?

What to do with Jesus. On a daily basis, in so many ways, we are confronted with the same challenge that confronted Pontius Pilate, governor of Judea, a man with a choice in the matter, a person of power. Do we do what the people want us to do with Jesus, what the popular trends say to do with Jesus, what the angry mob says to do with Jesus? Or do we get to know Jesus for ourselves and treat him like the Son of God, the lover of our souls, the Savior of the world, the forgiver of our sins? What to do with Jesus—that's the challenge that once confronted Pilate, and it's the challenge that confronts us daily.

Knowing Jesus

Another problem for Pilate was that he probably didn't know that much about Jesus. "Pilate asked him, 'Are you the king of the Jews?'" (Luke 23:3). It's likely that Pilate wasn't all that concerned with such a person anyway. Had Jesus truly been a threat, Pilate would have heard about him by now. And Pilate surely wasn't interested in some religious fanatic roaming the countryside forgiving people caught in the very act of their sins. He didn't know much about Jesus, and probably he didn't care to know. And that may be true for some of us as well. Some of us go to church all the time and still don't know much about who Jesus is because we're not really listening to the Scripture lessons or the sermons, or we're not reading the Bible on our own or attending a Bible study to find out more about who Jesus is and what he stands for.

Some people, if they ever found out some of the things that Jesus stands for and what he calls us to do, might ask to have their church membership revoked. "I didn't sign up for that. I didn't know he was like that." Some people know that the Bible contains commandments and laws and ethics by which God directs our behavior, but they'd be disappointed to learn that Jesus didn't come to throw out those parts of the Bible: "Do not think that I have come to abolish the law or the prophets; I have come not to abolish but to fulfill" (Matthew 5:17). They know that the Bible condemns adultery, but they'd be shocked to learn that Jesus condemns even a lustful look at someone else's spouse (Matthew 5:28). They know that it's wrong to murder someone, but they'd be astonished to learn that Jesus says that even anger or insults toward someone can bring judgment down on you (Matthew 5:22). Jesus took the punishments of the law for us, but he still wants us to act right, to live right, to treat each other and ourselves with the respect befitting children of the Most High God. Jesus said, "Unless your righteousness exceeds that of the scribes and Pharisees, you will never enter the kingdom of heaven" (Matthew 5:20). Some people really don't know Jesus.

We need to know Jesus. And the way we get to know Jesus is by walking with him, talking with him, listening to what he has to say about himself. And the way we do that is by reading the Bible for ourselves, going to Bible study, asking questions of the Bible, digging deep for answers, not just taking things at face value but really desiring to get to know who Jesus is. Spend some time in prayer with him. Spend some time in silent meditation listening for the voice of God. Maybe Jesus will turn out to be someone different than you expected. Maybe he won't be the Savior we wanted, but he will be the Savior we need, the Savior of the world, the answer for our troubles, the healer of our souls. Get to know Jesus. Take the time to get to know him. For to know him is to love him. To love him is to serve him. To serve him is to live for him. And to live for him is to praise him with every breath and every step of our lives.

The Truth about Jesus

Let's look at another problem that Pilate had. Luke reports, "They began to accuse him, saying, 'We found this man perverting our nation, forbidding us to pay taxes to the emperor'" (Luke 23:2). Whoa, now! It's bad enough that some folks don't really know who Jesus is and are forced to make decisions based on a Jesus they don't really know, but it's gone from bad to worse when people start telling a pack of lies about him. Jesus went about doing good, healing those oppressed by the devil, opening the eyes of the blind, making the cripple to walk, raising the dead back to life. In what way, shape, or form was that perverting the nation? He called on people to clean up their act, for vendors to stop ripping off others in the temple, for people to give to the emperor what was rightfully his. How was that perverting the nation? He never called for a violent overthrow of the Roman government, he never committed murder during a revolt like Barabbas did, and he even discouraged his own disciples from taking up weapons against the authorities. How was that perverting the nation? They were lying about Jesus.

And we must be very careful, because Pilate isn't the only one listening to lies about Jesus. Pilate isn't the only one hearing people say that our Lord is perverting the nation, that he's a threat to our society's freedoms, that he's backward, old-fashioned, out of touch. Those who accused Jesus before Pilate weren't the first group to make up lies about Jesus, and they aren't the last. Some people say that you can't embrace a sophisticated education and still be a Christian. They'll tell you that science proves that God doesn't exist, that Jesus didn't rise from the grave. They'll tell you that Christianity is the number-one problem with the world. Lies, lies, and more lies! Watch out, because you don't want to let your perspective on Jesus be formed by people who don't love Jesus, who don't know Jesus, and who tell lies about Jesus.

These same people never have anything good to say about Jesus' church either. They never give the church its due for being the backbone of the community, for providing services to the community, for reaching out to the community. Following Christ's teaching (Matthew 25:36), the church visits prison inmates, and people who receive Christ as their Lord and Savior while in prison have much lower rates of recidivism than do other prisoners.[1] And urban youth who make a commitment for Christ are more likely to go on to college.[2] Don't believe the smears that some people want to spread about Jesus and his church. People lied about Jesus to Pilate, who was trying to get to know him so that he could make an informed decision, and folks are lying about Jesus now.

A Decision about Jesus

Perhaps most troubling about Pilate's final action is that after being pressured to make a quick decision about Jesus, after not knowing much about Jesus, and after being lied to about who Jesus really was, Pilate still had a clear perspective about Jesus' innocence. "Pilate then called together the chief priests, the leaders, and the people, and said to them, 'You brought me this man as one who was perverting the people; and here I have examined him in your presence and have not found this man guilty of any of your charges against him'" (Luke 23:13-14). Pilate knew that Jesus hadn't done anything that this angry mob had accused him of doing. He knew that Jesus was not a threat to lead a military revolt, that he would not try to dissuade people from paying taxes. Pilate knew that Jesus wasn't deserving of the horrendous treatment that they were demanding. He saw Jesus as a good person, a kind person, an innocent person. But he did not see Jesus as God's Son, and so, despite whatever else he may have known, he handed Jesus over as they wished. The Scripture doesn't describe Pilate's emotional reaction, as it does that of the rich man who rejected Jesus and went away sad (Matthew 19:22). Historians debate whether Pilate took his own life at some point later that decade.[3] But in any event, we have to wonder if Pilate was saddened because of how he perceived Jesus as innocent but rejected him anyway.

I wonder how many there are who know enough about Jesus but are missing out on eternal life, on true peace and joy, by just the distance from head to heart. I wonder how many of us have the Pilate perspective: we know enough about Jesus, maybe not as much as we could but enough to know who he is, but when push comes to shove, when we're pressured to decide to follow him, to choose him, to do what he wants and what he did, to love our neighbors, to serve others, to give to those who ask of us, to befriend those in our society who need us instead of those that we think we need, we turn away from him. How many of us, every day, are in the same situation as Pilate, viewing the same Jesus, being challenged by these same raucous crowds? What will we do? Will we not only see Jesus for who he is, but also open up our hearts and let him in, let him be our Lord, let him be the ruler of our lives, our life coach, our mentor, our personal trainer, our role model, our pastor? Or do we have the Pilate perspective, where we know that we ought to give our life to Jesus, but instead we do what everybody around us wants?

Don't make the same mistake that Pilate made. Don't be fooled by the crowds and the pressures of this world. This is your opportunity to make a decision about what to do with Jesus in your life. Will you sentence him to death in your life, and crucify him all over again? Or will you invite him into your heart?

Cross Examinations

1. How do you handle this question on a daily basis: What should I do with Jesus?
2. In what ways have you attempted to know more about Jesus in the past year?
3. What lies about Jesus or the church have you heard recently, and how did you respond to them?

Notes

1. One report states that graduates of the InnerChange Freedom Initiative for prisoners "are significantly less likely to be either arrested or incarcerated during the two-year period following release from prison," and that this "represents initial evidence that program completion of this faith-based initiative is associated with lower rates of recidivism of former prisoners (http://www.demossnewspond.com/ifi/preliminary/Excerpt3.htm [accessed August 2, 2007]).

2. George Barna, *Transforming Children into Spiritual Champions* (Ventura, CA: Issachar Resources, 2003).

3. A. N. Sherwin-White, "Pilate, Pontius," *International Standard Bible Encyclopedia,* vol. 3, ed. G. W. Bromiley (Grand Rapids: Eerdmans, 1982), 867.

9

A Revelation of Mixed-Up Priorities
(Matthew 27:15-23)

So after they had gathered, Pilate said to them, "Whom do you want me to release for you, Jesus Barabbas or Jesus who is called the Messiah?"

(Matthew 27:17)

Maybe you hadn't noticed it before: there's more than one Jesus in the Bible. The Hebrew name "Yeshua" (from which we get "Joshua") means "The Lord will save,"[1] and besides being Jesus' name, it was also the name of one of his ancestors. Use of the name "Jesus" for people in Anglo-American culture is virtually unknown, perhaps out of reverence for it. In Hispanic culture, however, "Jesus" is a common name that even gets parsed out into nicknames such as "Jesse" and the playground name "Chuy."

Does it make you uncomfortable to hear the name "Jesus" coupled with the name "Barabbas," the name of our Lord joined with the name of an outlaw? If so, you will well understand how the Western world might have desired for that first part of Barabbas's name to be stricken from the Gospel record. The West was uncomfortable with the notion that the name of our Savior, the holy and innocent sacrificial Lamb of God, could be shared by someone who, as the Gospels attest, was a murderer and a bandit. But several ancient manuscripts and the early church father Origen note the name as it appears translated in the New Revised Standard Version: "Jesus Barabbas."[2]

The crowd chose Jesus Barabbas over Jesus the Christ. And as you know, our choices say something about ourselves. If I mention the jury in the O. J. Simpson trial, virtually every reader of this book who was alive at the time will have an opinion about why that jury found Simpson not guilty, what that verdict said about that jury. Your mind probably is already racing to what you thought about that jury, or what you thought about your friends' opinions on the verdict. Many people surmised that a mostly black jury would never convict a black man, despite the fact that black juries do so every day in courtrooms across America. And many people had convicted O. J. Simpson in their minds before he was even arrested, and that revealed something about them too, something a little more ugly and hidden than a whole lot of other sinful things that we see in this world. The decisions that we make reveal something about us, about our character, about our values, and they *do* reveal our priorities.

As we look at the story of Jesus' passion in Matthew's Gospel, we all quickly ascertain, I am sure, that the crowd and the religious leaders rushed to the wrong conclusion in choosing Barabbas, and we are satisfied with that as part of the redemption story long before prophesied by Isaiah, that people would despise and reject God's Christ. But if we examine the circumstances of the decision-making process that day, if we analyze the crowd and the leaders who demanded the ultimate punishment for our Lord, we will see that their decision to free the Jesus called Barabbas and to crucify the Jesus called the Christ reveals something crucial about the crowd: their priorities were all wrong. Jesus came to die for them, and they chose Barabbas. Jesus left his heavenly habitation to be born in the form of a man, to suffer, bleed, and die for the sins of this very crowd, and they chose Barabbas. Jesus was the Son of God, the healer of diseases, the raiser of the dead, the forgiver of sins, and they chose Barabbas. Talk about mixed-up priorities!

And I'm sorry to say that this same mixing up of priorities is prevalent in our own culture, in our own people, and in our own families sometimes: some people are choosing someone or something else over Jesus, choosing some cheap imitation of Jesus instead of the biblical, historical, Savior of the world.

The Hometown Favorite

What did those people know about Jesus Barabbas, and how was it that they could even think of setting free a man whom the Gospel writers identify as a murderer and a bandit? Well, Jesus Barabbas had a rather intriguing name. While the name "Jesus" in Hebrew is "Yeshua" and means "The Lord will save," the name "Barabbas" means "son of his father" or maybe even "son of a rabbi."[3] Barabbas may have been a preacher's kid! Doesn't that conjure up the image of a trouble-making teenager sneaking around behind his parents' back on Saturday night and then sitting dreary-eyed in church on Sunday morning while his father or mother stands in the pulpit railing against the ills of our society?

But more than that, we must look at the name "Barabbas" in light of Paul's letter to the church at Rome, where Paul said that because we are now in Christ, we have a different relationship with God and can refer to God as "Abba," meaning "Father." The sentiment expressed in Paul's writing and in the meaning of the term "Abba" is that of a rather intimate relationship between father and child, like a favorite child, the one whom everybody loves best.[4] There are those whom our society refers to as a "favorite son," a "homegrown boy," like NBA stars Rasheed Wallace and Aaron McKie, who may play ball for other cities now but still have fans in their native Philadelphia. We might understand Barabbas in a similar way, as someone whom the crowd that day knew well, someone from their 'hood or barrio. Barabbas was a "homie," and when the chance came to spring him from his jail cell, the crowd apparently leapt at the opportunity. Jesus the Christ was done in by some home-court officiating, by the home-court advantage. Being from Nazareth in Galilee, Jesus had one strike against him already. Jerusalemites did not have high regard for folks from up north in Galilee, to put it mildly. And even though Jesus had done wonderful, miraculous things for the people, this crowd wanted their boy instead.

This "hometown favorite" syndrome can also take place at the family level. Today there are parents who let their children gain control of home life and the decision-making process. Some parents choose to be popular with their children instead of obedient to their God. Some parents don't want to be the "bad guy," so they give in to their children's demands instead of obeying God's commands. And it's happening all over the country, with children turning into little monsters—spoiled, selfish, rude, irreverent, disrespectful, undisciplined. Now, I'm not the perfect parent, and my own children are far from perfect, but what am I supposed to think when I take my young daughter to a playground to ride on the swing, and some fourteen-year-old boy who wants to use that particular swing just grabs it and tells my daughter to get off? Who is raising this boy to think that he should take whatever he wants whenever he wants? Who is choosing to give this kid a sense of entitlement instead of instilling in him a love of sharing, a knowledge of what's right and wrong, an awareness that the world doesn't revolve around any individual? It's a revelation of mixed-up priorities.

In a sense, this "hometown favorite" syndrome can even be seen at the interpersonal level. When I was single, I always wanted to be with someone who was the most beautiful and popular. I remember one time when my future sister-in-law told me that I had mixed-up priorities when it came to finding a spouse, that how someone looks on the outside shouldn't be chosen over what that person believes on the inside. Are we choosing a mate based on how well she fills out a pair of tight jeans, or how much his biceps stretch the sleeves of his t-shirt, or how far you can get on the first date? Those are not the kind of criteria that we should use for making such a crucial decision. If they are, then our priorities are all mixed up. What about other criteria? Does this person go to church, read the Bible, show generosity and kindness to others, want to please God? Whom are you choosing today and why? It's a revelation of your priorities.

Politically Correct

Politics also came into play in the selection of Jesus Barabbas over Jesus the Christ. In mentioning that Barabbas was a murderer and a bandit, the Gospel writers were describing a man who had taken part in an uprising against the Roman government. Barabbas was of the school of thought that the only way for the Jews to effect political change was to use violence and force of arms against the Roman conquerors.[5] Any occupied or oppressed people will have those who believe that violent revolt is the best way. Some years ago, when I was in school, Stokely Carmichael came to Princeton and raised a ruckus when he refused to denounce the motto, coined by Malcolm X, "By any means necessary," meaning the use of violence. Barabbas would have liked that motto, and he would have been a good patriot in the American Revolution, because he thought like they thought, that violence was the best way to get their freedom. Indeed, as even Martin Luther King Jr., who advocated nonviolence, recognized, freedom is never voluntarily handed over by the oppressor but rather must be demanded by the oppressed.[6] And whether or not any of the crowd that day had ever taken part in an insurrection, they shared Barabbas's hatred of the Roman government and his desire to see vengeance taken. So when the opportunity came to choose between Jesus Barabbas, who shared their political philosophy, and Jesus the Christ, who rendered to Caesar the things that were Caesar's, when it was a choice between the politics of destroying your enemies or the theology of loving your enemies, the crowd chose the man who was "politically correct."

Someone once asked me why I don't have famous politicians in the heat of their races coming to speak in our church. I tell them, "It's not my priority." When they tell me that I could make a name for myself in the city if I had a certain candidate for office speak in my pulpit, I tell them that it's not my priority. When they tell me that I could rub elbows with some well-known senator or representative, I tell them that it's not my priority. I once went to the Hispanic prayer breakfast in Washington D.C., with various political figures from parties in attendance. During one of the speeches, I snuck out to look for a buffet table and accidentally bumped into Senator Joe Lieberman, who was talking with a Hispanic voter who had a camera and wanted a photograph with the senator. I apologized, and he said, "That's okay, but can you take a picture of us?" So I did. And when I finished taking the picture, a dozen people were lined up with their cameras wanting to have their picture taken with the former vice-presidential candidate. So I obliged. When we were done, the senator asked me if I wanted a picture for myself, and I said, "That wasn't my priority." Finding the buffet table was my priority.

My job is pastor of the Second Baptist Church of Germantown, not ward leader of the Democratic Party, or chairperson of the Young Republicans, or *jefe* of the Congreso Hispano. And with my job come certain requirements, foremost of which is the proclamation of the gospel of Jesus Christ. It is my job to preach that Christ Jesus came to save sinners. I do not preach the virtues of any politician, because no politician of any background can save sinners from their sins. Only Jesus can do that. We can gain enormous political power, we can have a booming economy, we can make the world safe for democracy, but what does it profit if we gain the whole world and lose our soul in the process? What good is it to have a politically free society that is captive to sin and lawlessness? What good is it to have civil rights if we can't behave in a civil manner toward each other, as Jesus taught when he said, "Love your neighbor as yourself"?

In your every political decision, are you first contemplating the will of God instead of the platform of your party? Are you willing to stand against the crowd but with your Lord and Savior when it is politically incorrect to have a faith conviction, to have a love for Jesus Christ, when others will think that you're not cool, not intelligent, not postmodern? What are your priorities? In your political determinations, are you using biblical values such as love and mercy and justice, Christlike principles such as turning the other cheek, loving your enemies, and advocating for the helpless? What are your priorities? Some people are afraid to voice an opinion that is out of step with their political party but in step with the Word of God. What are your priorities? Some people want to be popular in political discussions at the office or at school instead of experiencing rejection, as Jesus did, for taking a stand in the perfect will of God. What are your priorities? I firmly believe that if Christians, both Republican and Democrat, would raise their voices when they're concerned with their party's direction on issues such as war, poverty, affirmative action, abortion, and faith-based initiatives, then neither party could remain the same. The church would be reshaping political parties instead of, as has been happening, the political parties reshaping the church.

Priorities, Priorities

The crowd in Jerusalem that day chose the hometown favorite instead of the suffering servant from Nazareth, the violent political insurgent instead of the humble, donkey-riding king. And it showed something about their mixed-up priorities. But do you know who else's priorities were on display that day in Pilate's courtyard? Take a look at Jesus. The crowd chose a false savior, Jesus named Barabbas, a good ol' boy, a member of their political party, and Jesus the Christ never said a word. That reveals something about his priorities. They shouted for him to be crucified, screaming it at the top of their lungs, and Jesus never lifted a finger in his own defense. That reveals something about his priorities. They would call him names, mock him, spit on him, and scourge him, and he would endure it and suffer it all the way to the cross. That reveals something about his priorities. They would pierce his hands and feet with nails, and stab his side with a spear, and he would ask his Father to forgive them. That reveals something about the Savior's priorities.

Have you ever endured something for someone you loved? Have you ever stayed up late at night with a sick child because that kid was your number-one priority? Have you ever prayed and prayed while your teenager was out on the streets, and you reacted to every emergency siren and car backfire, because that kid was your number-one priority? I remember going to the hospital with one of my church members in the middle of the night because the doctors said that her husband wasn't going to make it and was quickly slipping away. We ran some red lights and rolled through some stop signs because obeying traffic signals was not our priority; getting to the hospital to be with her husband one more time was priority number one.

The crowd in Jerusalem that day had mixed-up priorities, but Jesus didn't. Did you know that you were on Jesus' mind that day, that you were his number-one priority? You are the apple of his eye. You are the love of his life. You are the reason he went through it all. You are the reason he gave his life. You are the reason he suffered and bled and died. Your life, your salvation, your future, your hopes, your loves, and your dreams were his priorities that day. He knew that without the shedding of blood there would be no remission of sins. He knew that all of us were lost in our trespasses. He knew that we were rebellious, that like sheep we had gone astray. He knew it. And it was his top priority to take your penalty and mine, to take your blame and mine, to take your suffering and mine. Jesus' actions that day revealed that his top priority was saving you and saving me.

Cross Examinations

1. What thoughts does the name "Jesus Barabbas" evoke in you?
2. In what ways have you chosen your culture over your faith?
3. What Christian teachings directly contradict those of your political party's platform?
4. In what ways does being a Christian conflict with being a member of your political party? Answer the same question in regard to your ethnic group, family, and job.

Notes

1. See R. P. Martin, "Jesus Christ," *International Standard Bible Encyclopedia,* vol. 2, ed. G. W. Bromiley (Grand Rapids: Eerdmans, 1982), 1034.

2. Michael J. Wilkins, "Barabbas," *Anchor Bible Dictionary,* vol. 1, ed. D. N. Freedman (New York: Doubleday, 1992), 607.

3. Ibid.

4. Ibid.

5. David Rhoads, "Zealots," *Anchor Bible Dictionary,* vol. 6, ed. D. N. Freedman (New York: Doubleday, 1992), 1043–54.

6. Martin Luther King Jr., *Letter from the Birmingham Jail* (San Francisco: HarperSanFrancisco, 1994).

10

Lessons from a Cross-Bearer
(Mark 15:16-24)

They compelled a passer-by,
who was coming in from the
country, to carry his cross;
it was Simon of Cyrene, the
father of Alexander and Rufus.
(Mark 15:21)

Cross-bearing is the practice of being unjustly and undeservedly singled out to endure a burden. For example, you're minding your own business, and one day someone decides to take you into slavery, or enact Jim Crow laws to intimidate you, or pass segregation laws to further limit you, or use you as a laboratory animal in a Tuskegee Experiment,[1] all for no other reason than the color of your skin. Going through that is cross-bearing.

Simon and Sons

Cross-bearing had its start with Simon of Cyrene, an African man. There is a strong presence of Africa in the Bible in general and in this text in particular. Cyrene was a city on the northern coast of Africa in the country called, in ancient and in modern times, Libya. In the centuries before and including the birth of Christ, Cyrene was known as the intellectual center of the ancient world, famed for its medical school, its philosophers, and a geographer named Eratosthenes, who before the time of Christ calculated the circumference of the world within fifty miles of what is accepted as correct today.

Two other Africans are mentioned in this text, Alexander and Rufus, Simon's two sons. The story of Simon is related in two other Gospels, Matthew and Luke, but only Mark mentions the names of Simon's two sons. And inquiring minds like mine want to know: Why is there no mention of Alexander and Rufus by Luke and Matthew, and why did Mark engage in what seems like an insignificant bit of name-dropping? But for name-dropping to be effective, the names must be familiar to those who are listening to you or, in this case, reading your Gospel. When I told my family in California that I met John Street (the mayor of Philadelphia) and shook his hand, they had no idea who in the world I was talking about. Name-dropping works only when the people you're talking to are impressed by the name. So when Mark dropped the names of Alexander and Rufus into his Gospel, it was because the audience that he was writing to knew these two men and probably thought highly of them.

The next question, then, is this: To whom was Mark writing? Most scholars think that Mark was writing to Romans and in Rome, where, it is believed, he was with Peter and was basing his Gospel account on that of Peter.[3] Now, besides the fact that Alexander and Rufus were the sons of Simon of Cyrene, what do we know about them? The apostle Paul, at the end of his letter to the Romans, where he is giving farewell instructions, writes, "Greet Rufus, chosen in the Lord; and greet his mother—a mother to me also" (Romans 16:13). And although the name "Rufus" was common in that day, most scholars believe that this Rufus of Mark's Gospel and the Rufus of Paul's letter were one and the same, that this Rufus must have been a well-known Christian, most likely a leader in the community (Paul calls Rufus "chosen in the Lord"), and that Paul was well acquainted with Rufus's family (Paul says that Rufus's mother is "a mother to me also"), perhaps because Paul had stayed with them during an evangelistic journey.[4] I know that this can happen, for in my youthful days as a traveling evangelist, I gained mothers all over the country with whom I stayed. Rufus, son of Simon the cross-bearer from Cyrene, is believed to have been a great Christian man, well known and well respected. That's why Paul greets him; that's why Mark name-drops him.

So Rufus became a great Christian leader.[5] With that in mind, let's turn our attention back to Mark's Gospel, where we are told that Simon of Cyrene, a passer-by, was compelled to carry Jesus' cross. There are some lessons from this first cross-bearer for us today. Consider for a moment what Simon might have been going through that day, what his experience was with the hated Roman soldiers when they singled him out, grabbed him from out of all the other people, and made him carry the heavy cross of a convicted felon who, it turned out, was the innocent Lord Jesus Christ. Here was Simon, in town to observe the Passover, minding his own business, when suddenly he becomes a recipient of the persecution being done to our Lord. I imagine that he must have been outraged to have been selected from the crowd for such a grueling and shameful task, and that this fueled his anger at the already hated Roman occupiers.

Maybe Simon was aware of the innocence of this man being crucified and was bitter at the Romans for their appalling treatment of Jesus, an innocent man falsely accused and put to death. Simon probably saw enough horrific inhuman behavior that day to scar his soul for life. The sight of Jesus being nailed to the cross, the casting of lots for his garments, the piercing of his side and the blood and water gushing forth, the gore and torment of a man dying a slow, agonizing death on a tree—all of this must have had an impact on Simon and on anyone who saw such things. People here in America have seen innocent loved ones put to death by savage racists who hung black men from trees. Some folks bear a cross placed on them by a racist society, by hundreds of years of slavery, by more years of discrimination and injustice. African Americans have been bearing a cross ever since there have been African Americans. Just like Simon the cross-bearer from Africa: unjustly persecuted, unfairly singled out, weighted down with a cross that slowed him down, keeping him from what he was doing. Simon may have been the first cross-bearer, but he certainly wasn't the last. What lessons can we learn from Simon?

Never the Same

One lesson is that once you have borne a cross, you are deeply affected, you are never the same. It will impact your life in some way, shape, or form. How did Simon, the first cross-bearer, manage his cross, and what is the comparison to how we are bearing ours? Did he consider all Romans to be devils because of their brutality and injustice toward himself and Jesus? Did he become an insurrectionist, like Barabbas and Judas Maccabeus, looking for ways to kill all Romans? Did he think that violent retribution was the only way to even the score for what the Romans had done and were doing? Did he remain mired in the bitterness and hatred that come with having been wronged? Maybe. But perhaps, instead, Simon saw how Jesus reacted to the situation. Maybe Simon saw so much love in this man Jesus that instead of rendering evil for evil, he decided to be like Jesus and return love for hatred. He saw Jesus' sacrifice on the cross, and he heard Jesus' words of forgiveness from the cross. Perhaps this was what stayed with Simon of Cyrene, the African cross-bearer, the father of Alexander and Rufus. Simon's experience could have driven him in either direction: toward hatred or toward love, toward revenge or forgiveness, toward bitterness and strife or love and mercy. Which would he choose? How would cross-bearing affect Simon of Cyrene, the father of Alexander and Rufus?

Setting an Example

A second lesson is that the manner in which you bear your cross will also have an impact on those around you, and it may well shape their future. Mark notes that Simon of Cyrene was the father of Alexander and Rufus. Rufus, we saw, turned out to be a notable Christian leader, a man acquainted with Paul and Mark, known throughout his community as a chosen man of God. Scripture does not tell us that Rufus was consumed with bitterness and hatred toward all things Roman. It does not tell us that Rufus was determined never to forget what evil his father had seen in Romans. Rather, it tells us that Rufus was a Christian. After all that their father had been through and seen firsthand, Alexander and Rufus had been brought up to be God-fearing Christian men who moved to Rome. Instead of hating Romans as those who persecuted their father, they spent their lives trying to win them to Christ. Simon's children wound up living in Rome and spreading the gospel there. That alone ought to tell us something about Simon of Cyrene. I imagine that had Simon been consumed with hatred and anger and bitterness and spite, his children would have been infected with the same virus of those debilitating sentiments. Apples don't fall far from their trees.

It is crucial that we set a good example for our children. They do pay attention to what we do and say. For example, the primary influence on whether or not young people will drink or smoke is whether or not their parents do so.[6] Young people will say to their parents, "I don't want to be like you." After all, kids say, parents are old school, not with it, not cool, out of touch. But soon enough, kids grow up, and they're acting pretty much like their parents. Young people will say, "I'll never raise my kids the way my parents raised me." But when they have children of their own, always in their subconscious thoughts is the question "What did my parents do for me in this situation?" And who is the first person they call when the baby is sick, when there's a problem? Mom or dad.

Married adults, haven't you experienced this? When you got married and were trying to figure out how to resolve conflict, how to communicate with your spouse, how to determine the roles of husband and wife, how to discipline your children, the first thing that went through your mind was "Well, my parents did it this way. This is what I'm used to." One of the lessons of cross-bearing is that somebody is watching you and will be like you. You are passing on traits to your children that you don't even realize. And that can be positive, but too often it is negative. If you disrespect or abuse your spouse, don't be surprised when your children do the same thing to their spouses or, just as sad, quietly accept mistreatment from their spouses. If you don't go to worship, don't give to the church, don't read the Bible, don't pray at home, don't love your neighbor, it's a good bet that your children will grow up to do likewise. But when you do put your faith into practice and work in Lord's vineyard with joy and gladness, you are setting an example that will not be forgotten. Your kids may rebel for a time—you can almost count on that!—but the promise is that in due season you will reap the harvest of the seeds that you've planted in them.

What happens when kids hear parents tell a joke that debases people because of the color of their skin or what country they're from? The kids may not be fully conscious of it, but they've just received authoritative instruction that some of God's children are not to be valued, honored, and loved. One of our problems in trusting people of other races is that our parents too often won't allow us to get beyond the horrible things of the past, won't allow us to forgive. I wonder if we can ever get to the point of understanding others not as those who have done us harm but as those who are brothers and sisters in Christ. Simon of Cyrene, the original African cross-bearer, could have raised his children to hate Romans, but instead his children turned out to love Jesus and to love Romans, as Jesus did. Simon passed on to his children not the hostility, outrage, mistrust, and anger but rather the forgiveness and the grace and the mercy of Jesus on the cross.

Learning to Forgive

A third lesson is that if we don't learn to forgive, that cross will wear us down and wear us out. Look at Simon as he looked at Jesus, an innocent man, beaten, bruised, crucified on a tree. See how Simon heard Jesus, hanging on the cross, say, "Father, forgive them; for they do not know what they are doing" (Luke 23:34). See how Simon decided that love, grace, and mercy were more powerful weapons than vengeance, bitterness, and hatred. See how Simon saw in Jesus the power of redemptive love, love that turns enemies into friends, that sets hatred and strife to flight, that leads historical rivals to be bound together. This is Jesus' love on that cross, the kind that loves you when you're wrong and when you're right; that loves you if you're black or if you're white and builds a bridge between the races; that can overcome injustice and unite us across divisions; that forgives past crimes and creates a new day based on hope. Simon of Cyrene, the father of Alexander and Rufus, is proof that our cross-bearing, practiced with forgiveness, strengthens us, builds up others, and shapes the future for the better.

You and I have the power to shape tomorrow. What lessons will we pass on to our children? What models will we show them? Certainly there are many good teachers from every area of human endeavor whose lessons we can and should pass along: George Washington Carver, Booker T. Washington, and Grover Washington Jr.; Harriet Tubman, Sojourner Truth, and Maya Angelou; James Cone, Cornell West, and Thurgood Marshall; A. Philip Randolph, Martin Luther King Jr., and Jesse Jackson. But I suggest that we not forget, and could do no better than, Simon of Cyrene, who teaches us about the far-reaching and blessed influence of cross-bearing.

Cross Examinations

1. How did Simon bear his cross, and what cross are you bearing for Christ?
2. Have you ever been the victim of oppression? If so, how did you respond?
3. Who is watching you and will emulate your behavior?
4. What legacy and lessons are you passing on to others?

Notes

1. In 1932, the Public Health Service, working with the Tuskegee Institute, began a study that has come to be known as the Tuskegee Syphilis Experiment. Some four hundred poor black men with syphilis from Macon County in Alabama were enrolled in the study, which sought to understand how the disease spreads and kills. The men were told that they were being treated for "bad blood." They were never treated for syphilis, even after penicillin became a standard cure for the disease in the late 1940s. For their participation, the men were given free medical exams, meals, and burial insurance. The experiment lasted for forty years, until public health workers leaked the story to the media in 1972.

3. William L. Lane, *The Gospel of Mark* (Grand Rapids: Eerdmans, 1974), 24.

4. Douglas J. Moo, *The Epistle to the Romans* (Grand Rapids: Eerdmans, 1996), 925.

5. C. N. Jefford, "Rufus," *International Standard Bible Encyclopedia*, vol. 4, ed. G. W. Bromiley (Grand Rapids: Eerdmans, 1982), 239.

6. George Barna, *Transforming Children into Spiritual Champions* (Ventura, CA: Issachar Resources, 2003), 83.

11

Surveying the Cross
(Luke 23:26-56)

> When they came to the place which is called The Skull, they crucified Jesus there with the criminals, one on his right and one on his left. (Luke 23:33)

I got a phone call one day from some folks conducting a survey about graduates of the University of Southern California. My ethnic background? Mexican. My line of work? Pastor. Then they asked my age and gave me three choices: 20–25, 26–35, and 36 or older. That's it—I'm officially over the hill!

From Luke 23:27 we get a sense of the large number of people who were there at the cross when Jesus was crucified. In surveying that crowd and those participating and/or victimized in the crucifixion of our Lord, I do believe that we might hear from heaven and proclaim the salvation that comes flowing from that place on Calvary known as "The Skull." A wonderful old hymn asks the question "Were you there when they crucified my Lord?" And it is in surveying the crowd, in these lives and their purposes for being there, in their backgrounds and in their personalities that we might be able to answer yes to that question and realize that although it took place two millennia ago, Jesus died on that cross for you and for me. So let us, in the spirit of another great hymn, survey that wondrous cross, for in doing so we will at once be convicted and encouraged, guilt-riddled and redeemed, included in the blame but excluded from our due punishment. We will realize that, yes, each and every one of us was there when they crucified our Lord.

Ethnic Groups

First, let's survey the diversity of ethnic groups at Jesus' cross. This idea differs from traditional Western European views, which typically portray nothing but white folks surrounding the cross of Christ. It's what we've seen in paintings, and it stains the glass of numerous cathedrals of the Western world. It occupies the pictures of our children's books. It might even be in your Bible somewhere in an artist's rendition. Ever since the time of the Renaissance, Western art has tended to depict the biblical world as being filled only with white, European-looking faces, leaving that image thoroughly imbedded in our mind's eye when it comes to surveying the cross.

But as we survey the cross through the eyes of Scripture, we see Simon from Cyrene, a place on the northern coast of Africa. And there were women from the mixture that formed the people of Israel, which included a line of people from the regions of modern-day Iraq;[1] the descendants of Moses, whose wife was a Cushite woman; and the descendants of Ephraim and Manasseh, whose mother was Egyptian. There were Italian soldiers, and Rome also had numerous foreign auxiliaries in its army. There was also a man named Jesus, and here is where we are most deluged with images from traditional Western artists, images that do not match the reality of how Jesus looked. Jesus, according to the genealogy in Matthew's Gospel, was a descendant of Rahab, a native of the region of Canaan and a woman of color. He was also a descendant of Ruth, a Moabite woman and, again, a woman of color. There are others in Jesus' lineage whom I could mention, but you get the idea: many, perhaps most, of the pictures of Jesus that we've seen throughout the years do not resemble how Jesus actually looked.

When I was in seminary, I made friends with people from different groups—rich and poor, blacks and whites, lovers of hip-hop and die-hard fans of country music. One day an argument got started about the color of Jesus. My African American friend said that Jesus was black because he was descended from people of color. My European American friend said that Jesus was white because all the artists' renderings of Jesus showed him as such. The argument carried on until they asked me what I thought. Lightening the mood, I said, "I think Jesus was Mexican. Who else names their children *Jesus*?"

Prior to the domination of Christianity by the European world, most artists' depictions of Jesus showed him as a black man.[2] The "Madonna with Child" that was so prevalent in ancient art depicted Mary and Jesus as Afro-Asiatic individuals. It was the Italian church that first took the liberty of drawing up a Jesus who had the skin pigmentation of its members, and then when the West engulfed Christianity, it became commonplace to understand Jesus as looking like a white man. Images of the black Jesus were systematically eradicated.

The fact is that there were a whole lot of different folks there at the cross. Jesus was crucified in Jerusalem during Passover, and the Pentecost story (Acts 2) shows that during such festivals Jerusalem was filled with people from all over the known world, people of all colors and ethnic backgrounds. And when Jesus died on that cross, he died for people all over the globe. Christianity is not a white-man's religion or a black-church institution. Jesus died for people of "every tribe and language and people and nation" (Revelation 5:9), people of every color and every ethnic group. He died in the presence of and on behalf of all of God's children.

Social Classes

Next, let's survey the classes of the people at Jesus' cross. Luke tells us that along with the low-ranking Roman soldiers, there was a Roman centurion. The soldiers were the blue-collar guys, the "grunts," but the centurion was in charge of one hundred soldiers.[3] So here we have a manager, a white-collar type. And Pontius Pilate, governor of Judea and a person of considerable political and military power, was in his fortress nearby, just several hundred yards from the cross. And there were women who followed Jesus from Galilee, a poor rural district, such that to be called "a Galilean" was a put-down. On top of that, in that culture these women had few rights and no power. And finally, on either side of Jesus were two people of another class, the criminal class. That's right, two thugs were there, societal outcasts reviled and sentenced to death by crucifixion.

They were all there at the cross of Jesus: the rich and the poor, the powerful and the powerless, the white collar and the blue collar, the lawmakers and the lawbreakers. Were you there too? Were you there when they crucified our Lord?

Emotional States

Next, let's survey some of the emotions that can be discerned from Luke's account of Jesus' cross. At Jesus' cross there were "women who were beating their breasts and wailing for him" (Luke 23:27). These women were in the throes of grief, watching as this innocent man who loved them went to his death. They were devastated by the hatred and jealousy of their religious leaders, by the sight of their shepherd being mistreated and disrespected. And there were those who mocked Jesus: "He saved others; let him save himself if he the Messiah of God, his chosen one!" (Luke 23:36); "If you are the King of the Jews, save yourself!" (Luke 23:37); even a man suffering the same painful execution spoke with contempt, saying, "Are you not the Messiah? Save yourself and us!" (Luke 23:39). These are the voices of cynics, people who had seen messiahs come and go and wouldn't be fooled again, skeptics who refused to believe in anything, especially that someone could be as good, loving, and just as Jesus. For them, Jesus couldn't be who he said he was, he couldn't be the Son of God. Then there's the centurion who watched the drama: how Jesus suffered, surrendered his spirit, and died; how at high noon darkness covered the whole land for three hours. The centurion's attitude was one of awe and belief, for when he saw what happened, "he praised God and said, 'Certainly this man was righteous'" (Luke 23:47).[4]

There was a wide range of emotions and attitudes on display at the cross of Jesus: sorrow and loss, cynicism and skepticism, wonder and faith. There were the emotionally wounded and the emotionally calloused, the skeptical mind and the open mind, the hardhearted and the tenderhearted. Were you there too? Were you there when they crucified our Lord?

Spiritual Conditions

Finally, let's survey some spiritual conditions at Jesus' cross. Luke speaks of "a good and righteous man named Joseph, who, though a member of the council, had not agreed to their plan and action" (Luke 23:50-51). There were righteous people there, to be sure. John, in his Gospel, tells us that both the mother of Jesus and John the beloved disciple were there. And the women whom Luke tells about who followed Jesus, who took care of him from their own limited funds (Luke 8:1-3), were faithful to him even in his death. They didn't turn tail and run when the going got tough. They did not abandon him when he needed them the most. They were righteous in spirit.

But also there were those whose spirits were seared with sin and hatred, who not only openly mocked the Lord but also participated in his demise. They mocked him, spat on him, teased him, and made fun of him; they whipped and wounded him, placed a crown of thorns on his head, nailed his hands and feet to the cross; they gave him vinegar to drink and pierced his side with a spear.

I heard about a seminary professor who was well known for his unusual and insightful teaching tools, which his students were always eager to see. One day, he told the class to take a piece of paper and draw a picture of someone they most would like to throw a dart at, and when they were done, he would pass out darts. The students thought about people who had hurt or betrayed them, or someone they disliked, or some politician whose policies bothered them. And then one by one they taped the pictures to the wall and took turns throwing darts at the images that they had created. Some were passionate and others laughed as they tore the paper, cutting the pictures of the faces, deforming them almost beyond recognition, and relishing their accomplishment. Then after the last dart had been thrown, the last injury to those faces had been inflicted, and the last derogatory remark had been uttered, the professor pulled down the wallpaper, which now was severely damaged by the darts. Behind those ruptured pictures and that damaged wallpaper was a picture of Jesus on the cross, now badly torn, filled with holes, filled with marks and wounds from the darts that the students had thrown. Then, in shock, these Christian men and women listened as the professor read aloud two Bible verses. "Inasmuch as you have done it to the least of these, you have done it unto me." And then, "Father, forgive them, for they know not what they do."

We All Were There

We are two thousand years removed from the scene at the cross, but we were there. You may be a baby boomer or from Generation X, Y, or Next. You may be a senior citizen or a high school senior, a yuppie or a buppie, a teeniebopper or a hip-hopper, but you were there. You may be a veteran of World War II or the Vietnam War, a Gulf War hero or a conscientious objector, but you were there. You may be weak or you may be strong, you may be right or you may be wrong, but you were there. You may be up or you may be down, you may have a smile or you may wear a frown, but you were there. Red, yellow, black, white—we all were within his sight. We were there.

No wonder Isaiah said "he was wounded for our transgressions, crushed for our iniquities; upon him was the punishment that made us whole, and by his bruises we are healed" (Isaiah 53:5). We were there. He died for you, and he died for me. "All we like sheep have gone astray; we have all turned to our own way, and the LORD has laid on him the iniquity of us all" (Isaiah 53:6). We were there. And sometimes, it causes me to tremble.

Cross Examinations

1. How has your church affirmed and invited people of different ethnic backgrounds?
2. What social classes are represented in your church, and how can your church work toward becoming a more inclusive congregation?
3. What can/does your church do for those who are dealing with grief, depression, and other emotional/psychological issues?

4. How does the knowledge of Jesus' inclusion of you at the cross affect your life?

Notes

1. A. R. Millard, "Abraham," *Anchor Bible Dictionary,* vol. 1, ed. D. N. Freedman (New York: Doubleday, 1992), 35–41.

2. Cain Hope Felder, ed., *The Original African Heritage Study Bible* (Nashville: James C. Winston, 1993), xiv.

3. T. Nicol, "Centurion," *International Standard Bible Encyclopedia,* vol. 1, ed. G. W. Bromiley (Grand Rapids: Eerdmans, 1982), 629.

4. The Greek word for "righteous," *dikaios,* can also mean "innocent."

12

Sinners in the Hands of a Suffering Savior

(Luke 23:32-43)

But the other rebuked him,
saying, "Do you not fear God,
since you are under the same
sentence of condemnation?"
(Luke 23:40)

The fear of God is a perennial topic of conversation among the people of God. Proverbs 9:10 says, "The fear of the LORD is the beginning of wisdom." And although the term "fear" refers to the proper respect that is due the eternal and all-powerful God, there is indeed an intimation that we should also respect God as we do the destructive power of a raging fire or a stormy sea. Throughout the Old Testament, God's wrath is often on display. We need only thumb through the first book of the Bible to find stories of discipline and destruction, condemnation and vengeance.

Edwards's Angry God

The title of this chapter plays on a sermon by Jonathan Edwards during the Great Awakening of the eighteenth century, which prompted a religious revival across the colonies. The title of that sermon, "Sinners in the Hands of an Angry God," conveys intimidating imagery on its own, and the sermon's language and illustrations are even more daunting and harrowing than the title. Preaching from Deuteronomy 32:35, which threatens God's vengeance on the unrepentant Israelites, who had frustrated God with their sin and unbelief, Edwards wrote:

Thus it is that natural men are held in the hand of God, over the pit of hell; they have deserved the fiery pit, and are already sentenced to it; and God is dreadfully provoked, his anger is as great towards them as to those that are actually suffering the executions of the fierceness of his wrath in hell, and they have done nothing in the least to appease or abate that anger. . . . In short, they have no refuge, nothing to take hold of; all that preserves them every moment is the mere arbitrary will, and uncovenanted, unobliged forbearance of an incensed God.[1]

Both Edwards's sermon and the Scripture on which it was based were intended to strike fear in the hearts of sinners regarding their fate if they dared not repent of the wicked deeds that have so angered God. That image of an angry God holding sinners over a fiery pit, demanding proper respect and behavior or else, was meant to change human hearts, and indeed this strategy had a moderate, if temporary, degree of success. The Great Awakening is a historical fact. Many people responded to the fear of God.

But in our text from the Gospel of Luke, we see a story of two criminals being crucified, nailed to a cross alongside an innocent man who was dying for the sins of the world, the Lord Jesus Christ, who had no sin. And apparently, the first criminal, as described in the Scripture and referenced by the second criminal, had no fear of God. Despite the dire circumstances and his own suffering and shame, this man "kept on deriding" Jesus (Luke 23:39). Even though he had been nailed to a cross for his crimes, he had no sense of remorse, no change of heart, no yearning to repent from his sins and turn from his evil and dastardly attitude. No, this first criminal was going to maintain his tough image, his rebellious attitude, his defiant tone of voice. That may be part of the reason that he was held that day over the fiery pit of hell by the hands of the Roman criminal-justice system. At the height of discipline, the apex of corporal punishment, this first felon continued to chime in with those others who derided our Savior, mockingly tempting him to come down from the cross. In so doing, this defiant criminal may well serve as a case in point of how such punishment is rather ineffective as a deterrent.

The World's Angry People

The issue of capital punishment has raged on throughout the centuries, but this man hanging on a cross demonstrates that as long as people are sinners, no measure of fear or punishment will serve to deter them. Sinners will be sinners. As a preacher of the forgiveness of sins, I'll always have a job, since there will always be sinners. Statistics on murder and other crimes are unchanged by the imposition of capital punishment, and yet there are those who insist on its implementation as a deterrent. It seems to me that rather than how Edwards phrased it, one might well need to be afraid of being a sinner in the hands of angry human beings. For when human beings get angry, crucifixions take place, lynchings and lethal injections and firing squads and electric chairs all come about.

Human beings get creative in their attempts to hold people over the fiery pit of hell. It's the strategy employed by terrorists around the globe, using suicide bombers and videotaped murders to hold the people of the United States in their angry hands and terrorize them into changing the foreign policies of their government and the freedom and decadence of their society. And for its part, the United States, like many other nations on earth, has used military force in the same manner, threatening death and destruction to those who refuse to repent from their hatred of the most powerful nation on earth. I wonder if it might be a human tendency to want to hold those who have wronged us in the palm of our hand and dangle them over a fiery death, insisting that they fear us, demanding that they respect us.

Look at our Scripture text, which shows three persons being ruthlessly killed on crosses so that passers-by might see their horrible fate and be deterred from similar crimes. Now, recall our prison system and its inmates on death row, and consider how vengeful human beings can be. Think about the people killed in the bombing of mosques by radical militants, or about the journalists beheaded by religious fanatics, and consider what it must be to be a "sinner" in the hands of an angry human being. And you don't need to go to the other side of the world to see it. Look down the streets of our own cities, where drug dealers assassinate their rivals and opponents, sending messages of fear to anyone who would challenge them in their odious business. See how gang members handle their enemies. See what goes on behind closed doors when an angry husband abuses his wife in an attempt to grab her and dangle her over the fire of physical harm until he gets what he sees as proper fear and respect.

Jonathan Edwards got everybody worked up over the thought of sinners in the hands of an angry God, but being in the hands of angry humanity isn't much better. Human beings take their wrath out with violence and warfare, with knives and guns and bombs, with weapons of mass destruction and acts of terrorism. And the effect of such vengeance, of such attempts to produce fear and respect in the hearts of others, has proven over the years to be entirely and irrefutably unsuccessful. After centuries of attempting to solve the world's problems with armies and weapons, we have more war and less peace. Instead of having more justice, we have more sin. Instead of having more love, we have more hatred. It just doesn't work!

God's Suffering Savior

But there is something that does work. Our Scripture depicts two sinners dying alongside the spotless Lamb of God, two sinners in the angry hands of the criminal-justice system, two sinners whose crimes were determined by the courts of law to be deserving of death, who were beyond repair, beyond redemption, who were incorrigible and of no good use to anyone. And there they hung, nailed to crosses, dying a cruel and unusual death. This first criminal, hanging on a cross adjacent to our suffering Savior, maintains his disregard for civility and continues defiant in his attitude toward God's Christ. Imagine yourself being right next to the dying Lamb of God, seeing up close and personal his suffering and shame for the sins of the world, knowing firsthand the pain that he was enduring because you were enduring it too, and yet still remaining insolent and disobedient. But then there is that second criminal, who, although guilty as charged of his crimes, admits his guilt and sins in the presence of the dying Savior and makes a last-ditch attempt at spiritual clemency.

Now, if we hold to the image from Edwards's sermon, we would think that the God who was angered by sinful human conduct would have no mercy. God dangling sinners over the pit of hell—an image of a God who isn't emotionally injured and wounded at being rejected by his own people but rather is consumed, as humans are, with revenge and anger. And perhaps many people today have this view of God—a punishing, merciless entity so much like the evil human beings of this world that it seems pointless to regard such a deity with any respect. After all, we get enough of that kind of anger from people right here, so why bother with a God like that? But the second criminal makes a sinking-ship prayer to Jesus hanging on the cross, so he must have had at least some shred of hope in and understanding of God that went beyond the angry, vengeful image of God that to this day haunts the imaginations of far too many.

When that second criminal, a guilty sinner deserving of death, appealed to Jesus with a last-gasp prayer, how did Jesus respond? What happened at that urgent moment, with little time to spare, when this sinner was in the hands of our suffering Savior? The criminal's cross tells us how the criminal-justice system responded to any pleas for clemency that he may have made. We know all too well how angry human beings often respond to petitions for forgiveness and redemption, how this world treats offenders in the clutches of its hands. But when this convicted criminal, this sinner, admitted his wrongdoing, expressed respect for God, and pleaded for leniency, for Jesus to remember him, when he placed his life in the hands of the King of kings, what happened? Did Jesus respond angrily, "You're getting what you deserve"? Did Jesus remind him of the old standard of an eye for an eye? Did Jesus cite chapter and verse of the law that this man had broken? As this criminal dangled there on the cross between life and death, between heaven above and hell beneath, admitting that he was wrong, acknowledging that he deserved such punishment, did Jesus respond with anger? Vengeance? Hatred?

This is important, because many of us have it in our minds that Jesus will respond to our sinfulness with acrimony. We don't like to talk about it in public, but we think that we're not good enough, that like this criminal we deserve our punishment, that we've messed up and can't make it right. "I can't turn back the clock," we say. "Oh well," we sigh, "I've made my bed, and I've got to lie in it." We think of Jesus as if he were no different from us, as unforgiving as we are when hurt, as vengeful as we are when wronged, as angry as we are when betrayed.

This matter is crucial. What happens when sinners finds themselves in the hands of our suffering Savior? What happens when we mess up and get caught by the watchful eye of an all-knowing God? What happens when we confess our sins? What happens when we ask God to remember us? Is this the God of anger and vengeance or of kindness and forgiveness? Is God overcome with thirst for punishment, or is God overflowing with mercy? Is God consumed with a fire of destruction or with love for creation? That criminal, that sinner, that flawed human being, that person who had let God down time and time again cried out to Jesus, certainly in all humility, "Jesus, remember me when you come into your kingdom." Jesus replied, "Truly I tell you, today you will be with me in Paradise" (Luke 23:42-43).

"Today," Jesus said. "Right now, it's all right. Right now, I love you. Right now, your sins are forgiven you. Right now, even though you waited until the last second, even though you messed up, even though you've blown it, even though you knew it was wrong and did it anyway. This day you will be with me. I won't leave you or forsake you. Just as you are, come to me."

No matter what you've done, no matter how angry you think God is at what you've done, no matter how angry *you* are at what you've done, you need to know that we are sinners in the hands of a suffering, forgiving Savior. I thank God that I'm a sinner in the hands of that Savior. Aren't you glad about it? Isn't Jesus your best and only hope? Don't people forsake you? Don't politicians break their word to you? Doesn't society abandon you? Doesn't the government turn its back on you? But rejoice and be glad, because Jesus won't forget you. Today, right now, Jesus remembers you, loves you, forgives you.

Cross Examinations

1. How does Jesus' forgiveness of the criminal on the cross impact your views on capital punishment?
2. What is your perception of Jonathan Edwards's sermon "Sinners in the Hands of an Angry God," and how has that shaped your view of Christ?
3. Have you known anyone who was thought to be beyond help, but whose life was totally changed when he or she came to Christ?
4. How has Christ's forgiveness of your sins affected how you treat the sins of others? Of those who sin particularly against you?

Note

1. Jonathan Edwards, "Sinners in the Hands of an Angry God," in *A Treasury of Great Preaching*, vol. 3, Clyde E. Fant Jr. and William M. Pinson Jr., eds. (Dallas: Word Publishing, 1995), 61.

13

Tempted to Leave the Cross*
(Matthew 27:39-44)

"You who would destroy
the temple and build it in
three days, save yourself!
If you are the Son of God,
come down from the cross."
(Matthew 27:40)

Athletes often are tested by opposing crowds that are trying to distract them from the goal. People frantically wave their arms and shout at the top of their lungs in an effort to break the athlete's concentration and force a mistake. A free-throw shooter facing the basket with the game on the line, a field-goal kicker standing forty-five yards away from the goalpost, a pitcher on the mound needing to throw one more strike—and in each case the opposing crowd is doing its level best to create a big enough distraction to prevent the athlete from reaching that goal.

In our Scripture text, Jesus had been nailed to the cross, and he was bleeding from the wounds in his hands and feet and from the crown of thorns on his head. He was hanging there, dying a gruesome death reserved for the vilest of criminals, when people began trying to distract him from his goal: the temptation to leave the cross came at him. Matthew tells us that there were folks

*For the ideas in this chapter I am indebted to Rev. Donald L. Grant and Rev. Dr. S. Howard Woodson Jr.

passing by who were not particularly involved in Jesus' situation. They were just looky-loos, "gapers" on the highway of life, people who didn't realize what was at stake for them in the cross of Christ, who cared nothing for his status as the Son of God and the Savior of the world. If it were today, they probably would have read an article about Jesus' case in the local newspaper or maybe have seen it on Court TV. They didn't care one bit about Jesus, but they had the audacity to throw sarcasm in his direction and mockingly tempt him: "If you are the Son of God, come down from the cross." Jesus could have considered the validity of their argument and thought that he had a duty to confirm his identity. After all, didn't he have an obligation to prove to those in doubt that he was indeed the Son of God? It seems like a righteous idea for an innocent man to come down from the cross. But he stayed there anyway.

Next we learn of another group of people, the chief priests along with the scribes and elders, contemporary rivals of Jesus who, for their own plotting and deceits against him, might well have deserved a cross of their own. They said, "He saved others; he cannot save himself. He is the King of Israel; let him come down from the cross now, and we will believe in him. He trusts in God; let God deliver him now, if he wants to" (Matthew 27:42-43). Imagine the temptation that may have flashed into Jesus' mind at that moment. "Here are some opponents who say that they will become my followers if I come down now. They are doubting my kingship over the people of God, and I can prove it to them simply by coming down from the cross." And it probably wouldn't have been that hard for Jesus to do. After all, Jesus had raised Lazarus from the dead after four days in the tomb. He had healed leprous skin, restored sight to blind eyes, calmed winds and waters of raging storms, fed thousands with a few loaves and fish. Coming down from the cross wouldn't even be his greatest miracle.

And if he does it, they say, they will believe in him. "Why don't you come down now, Jesus? You're so great, so holy, so righteous. Why don't you come down now? We'll believe in you. We'll join your group. We'll stop picking on you and persecuting you and stirring up trouble against you if you just come down from the cross now. Why don't you come down now?" But Jesus stays there all the while, never uttering a word to them, never speaking up to correct their misstatements and falsehoods, never debating the sincerity of their bargaining tactics, never challenging the false charge that he saved others but couldn't save himself. It wasn't that he *could* not save himself, but rather that he *would* not. He could have summoned thousands of angels to help him. He could have performed any miraculous display that he wanted. "Why don't you come down now, Jesus?"

We're all tempted at times to do this very thing, to leave the cross of Christ, to disdain our calling and our election by God and turn our lives over to the whim and will of societal mandates. We're tempted every day to turn our backs on the way God has called us to live, on the things God has called us to do, on the commandments God has given us to follow, and on the message God has called us to proclaim. We're tempted every day to take our focus off of what Jesus did for us and think instead of what our educations or careers or social groups have done for us. I look at Jesus being tempted by these folks, and I imagine what those tempters must have thought were Jesus' vulnerabilities that would make him susceptible to yielding to their temptation. And if *he* was vulnerable, think how much more so we are vulnerable to the temptation to leave the cross.

The Popular Thing to Do

Jesus might have been tempted to leave the cross because it would have been the popular thing to do. Everybody wanted him to do it. Those who passed by derided him and said, "Let him come down from the cross now, and we will believe in him" (Matthew 27:42). You and I are tempted every day by a culture that says that it will come to church if we change what we're preaching, a culture that is increasingly contradicting the teaching of the Scriptures, the Scriptures that have been proclaiming truth, justice, righteousness, love, faith, and hope for thousands of years. How arrogant this generation is. They are tempting us to do and preach what everybody else is finding so popular, to conform this gospel to the culture instead of conforming this culture to the gospel. We're tempted to follow whatever the church-growth gurus say will increase our attendance, or whatever the long-standing members think will maintain our stature in the community, or whatever the younger crowd thinks is cool these days. We're tempted to leave the cross.

"Preachers," Dr. Howard Woodson said, "are tempted to preach about anything under the sun *other* than the cross of Christ," anything other than his call for repentance from sin, other than his grace, mercy, love, and faith. We're tempted to preach that Jesus' death on the cross wasn't to atone for our sins but rather to condone our sins. We're tempted to preach popular doctrines to ears itching to hear them, to be trendy and in style with the fads and fashions of the day, instead of preaching the shame, reproach, suffering, bewilderment, grace, love, and power of the cross of Christ. We're tempted to leave the cross in exchange for being more popular with our members, or to gain prestige in the community, or to win an invitation to the mayor's house or the state house or the White House by saying "the right things" about hot topics. We're tempted by book deals and teaching jobs and speaking engagements to preach some other gospel, one that's more in keeping with the times than with the Word, more in line with Hollywood's view of things than with heaven's view of things.

And the devil will make you think that if you don't start preaching and living the way that the world wants you to, protest groups will line up outside your church door. News media will run pieces on how you are intolerant to certain groups because you believe that Christ died to redeem people from sin instead of just excusing their sins. And we worry about it and are tempted by it: to be in good standing with this fallen world, to stray from the cross of Christ in order to stay in the good graces of a sinful culture. Holding to the conviction of the cross of Christ is a lonely road to travel sometimes. Jesus was tempted to leave the cross because it was the popular thing to do.

Youthful Inexperience

Jesus also might have been tempted because of his youthful inexperience. Jesus was only about thirty years old when he began his ministry and thirty-three when he went to the cross. He grew up in rural Galilee and hadn't experienced much of the wider world; if he were to die here and now on the cross, he might regret missing out on so much of life.

Young people especially are being tempted to leave the cross today. The world is offering many enticements to them. Everywhere you turn, someone is tempting them to leave the teachings of the Scriptures, to lure them away from being a Christian, to undermine the solid foundations of faith and holiness that the church is trying to establish for them. When someone says to you, "Come on, everybody is doing it," offering drugs and alcohol, or premarital sex, or a way to cheat in school, or an invitation to gang violence, you're being tempted to leave the cross. Don't do it. Jesus died on that cross for you. He suffered and bled and died for you so that you wouldn't know the suffering, blood, and death of drug addiction, sexual diseases, drunk driving, and gang violence. Yes, you're tempted, but hang in there with Jesus. The temptations may indeed look good and seem to have no consequences; it may seem that no one will ever find out, that nobody's going to get hurt. But what they don't tell you on the street corner is that freewheeling sexual adventures will get you killed; joining a gang to act tough and be cool will get you killed; sticking a needle in your arm to get high will get you killed. Keep your eyes on Jesus. He hung in there for you, so you hang in there for him. He died for you so that you could live for him. Don't turn your back on the man who gave his life for you. Don't leave the cross.

The temptation came to a young married man who was reared in the church, married in the church, and had small children being raised in the church. And then it came at him, hard, that he hadn't sampled all that the world had to offer, that he was missing out on something, that he'd been with only one woman and wanted more. He was tempted to leave the cross, and when he did, he lost his wife and his house, had to pay alimony, and needed a court order just to take his kids to a baseball game. All because he left the cross. Don't do it, young single people. Don't do it, young married people. You're tempted to leave the cross, but don't buy into what the world is offering in its place.

Not the Way He Wanted

Jesus also might have been tempted to leave the cross because things didn't go the way he wanted. Jesus had prayed, "My Father, if it is possible, let this cup pass from me" (Matthew 26:39). He had cried out from the cross, "My God, my God, why have you forsaken me?" (Matthew 27:46). When God doesn't answer prayers the way we'd like, we're tempted to throw in the towel, to give up hope, to lose faith, to leave the cross. When we can't understand the whys and wherefores of what God does, we're tempted to leave the cross. Pastors find themselves in that spot sometimes, wondering why their new church program flopped, why their ministry doesn't measure up to those of other pastors, why they make much less money than their college classmates who went on to something other than theological school. They're tempted to leave the cross.

When my brother, Rev. Paul Flores, received his doctorate, I attended the ceremony. I looked through the program for his name, and when I found it, I saw his full name: "Paul Angel Flores." "Angel" is the name of my mother's oldest brother, who died in World War II. And I was immediately reminded of the story of how my grandmother Licia Chavez was in constant prayer for her son Angel as he fought in that war. My uncle Ernie told me that she constantly quoted from Psalm 91: "He shall give his angels charge over thee, to keep thee in all thy ways. They shall bear thee up in their hands, lest thou dash thy foot against a stone" (Psalm 91:11-12 KJV); and, "A thousand shall fall at thy side, and ten thousand at thy right hand; but it shall not come nigh thee" (Psalm 91:7 KJV). And then one day the telegram came notifying her that her firstborn son had been killed at the Battle of the Bulge. You can imagine what horror swept through her soul, and you might also wonder if that was an opportunity for the devil to tempt her to forsake her faith, to be angry at God, to give up. But that night, the very night when she learned of her son's death, there was a church revival meeting, and my grandmother was the worship leader. And that night, although no one expected her to do so, my grandmother went to church to worship the Lord. Everyone else was confounded at her faith in the midst of grief, but she was going to worship the Lord. I don't know what songs she led that night, but I can imagine her waving her uplifted arms to the Lord and singing, "Tu fidelidad es grande" ("Your faithfulness is great"), or "Te vengo a decir te alabo Señor, te adoro Señor" ("I come to tell you I praise you, Lord, I worship you, Lord").

Have you ever lay awake all night wondering what happened, why God hasn't done what you expected, what you know God can do and believed that God should do? Family conflict, serious illness, financial trouble, and God hasn't answered your prayer yet. And sometimes we put God to the test, challenging God to either do our bidding or watch us turn our backs. Let me tell you something: prayer is not meant to change God, but to change us. Prayer isn't about getting God to do our bidding, but about getting us to do God's bidding. Prayer shouldn't say to God, "Do it my way," but rather, as the old hymn puts it, "Have thine own way, Lord." We don't, and we shouldn't, always get what we want. Life is not like some fast-food restaurant with God sitting at the drive-up window taking our prayer orders. And many people, when they realize this, when they realize that God is in charge and not at our beck and call, are tempted to leave the cross. They'll say, "It's too hard, hanging on to the cross. It's too painful and too lonely. It's an anguish that is unimaginable." And when they can't understand where God is, when they cry out, "My God, my God, why have you forsaken me?", when their hearts are broken and their lives are shattered, when their families are grieving and their friends are bewildered, they'll be tempted to leave the cross.

On the Cross, Out of the Grave

Jesus could have answered his tempters, "If I come down now, it may be culturally popular, but that's not why I came. If I come down now, it may be personally gratifying, but that's not why I came. If I come down now, I can shut the mouths of these hypocrites and liars who dictate popular opinion, but that's not why I came. If I come down now, I may receive applause from people all over the world, but that's not why I came. No, I came to seek and save that which is lost. I came to bring good news to the oppressed. I came to bring healing to the brokenhearted. I came to proclaim release to the captives. I came to declare the acceptable year of the Lord. I came to comfort mourners, to provide for those who mourn in Zion, to give them a garland instead of ashes, the oil of gladness instead of mourning, the mantle of praise instead of a faint spirit. I came to seek and save that which is lost.

"If I come down now, it will be too soon. I've still got to make captivity captive. I've still got to rip the veil of temple from top to bottom. I've still got to get the keys to death, hell, and the grave. I've got to write redemption's story.

"If I come down now, it will be too soon. I've got to suffer, bleed, and die. I've got to lay down my life so that I can take it up again. I've got to pay for the remission of sins. I've got to give my life as a ransom for all God's children.

"If I come down now, it will be too soon. Some young man is about to inject a filthy syringe full of heroin into his arm.

"If I come down now, it will be too soon. Some young lady is thinking about selling her body to buy groceries for her kids.

"If I come down now, it will be too soon. Some couple are destroying their marriage and think that they're beyond help.

"If I come down now, it will be too soon. A city neighborhood is becoming a war zone, the devil is having a field day, God's people are perishing, souls need saving.

"If I come down now, it will be too soon."

Jesus was tempted to leave the cross, but he didn't. He hung there that Friday morning, with the sun turning to blood, with darkness covering the face of the earth. He hung there while the veil of the temple was torn from top to bottom. He hung there while they pierced him in his side and blood and water gushed out, confirming that he had finally given up his spirit.

They took him down from that cross—Joseph of Arimathea and the women—and they placed him in that tomb and sealed it up with a stone. And there he lay all Friday afternoon, and he lay there all Friday night; and he lay there all day Saturday, and he lay there all Saturday night.

But early Sunday morning, he arose. He arose as if to say, "Now is the day of salvation. If you hear God's voice, do not harden your hearts." He arose saying, "Now is the time to take the keys to death, hell, and the grave." He arose saying, "Now it's all right. Now it's time. Now captivity can be made captive. Now sinners can be transformed into saints. Now death can be swallowed up by life. Now there is hope of the resurrection. Now!"

Cross Examinations

1. In what ways have you been tempted to leave the cross?
2. What new teachings are fashionable in our contemporary culture but stand in contrast to the teachings of the Bible?
3. Who in your life has served as an example of someone who remained faithful to God through trials and troubles?

14

The Closer I Get to You

(John 19:25)

Standing near the cross of
Jesus were his mother, and his
mother's sister, Mary the wife
of Clopas, and Mary Magdalene.
(John 19:25)

There is perhaps no verse of Scripture that better depicts how much commitment, how much loyalty, how much love for the Son of God we are called to maintain and display, than does John 19:25. At the end of a Gospel filled with miracles and healings and a parade where a throng of people heralded Jesus as the expected Messiah, it all came down to just these faithful few standing near the cross of punishment and execution on a hill far away. Gone were the shouters of his messiahship. Gone were the thousands who ate the plentiful bread and fish that he provided and who then devoured the rich word of his teachings. Now, at the cross, even most of his chosen disciples are gone. It's down to four women and, we are told, "the disciple whom he loved" (John 19:26).

Words of prophecy and prediction, quoted by Jesus, had turned into cold, stark reality: "I will strike the shepherd, and the sheep will be scattered" (Mark 14:27). Never mind how many times the shepherd had rescued the sheep, or how much the shepherd had done by providing daily food for the sheep, or how great were the love and devotion that the shepherd had for the sheep. It is the very nature of the sheep to scatter when the shepherd is smitten, to run off and forget who the shepherd is and what the shepherd has done. So it was with the followers of Jesus then, and so it is with the followers of Jesus now.

Keeping Our Distance

It's not all that difficult to ascertain the reasons or to understand the motives of those who wanted to put some distance between themselves and this now-convicted criminal and political pariah named Jesus. For Peter, who stood at a distance during the trial of Jesus, it was a matter of self-preservation. It was no longer a good idea to identify yourself as one of Jesus' disciples. We understand. At one time, not that long before, people had come to Peter and begged him to let Jesus touch their children. Some of them wanted Peter and the other disciples to pray for them the way Jesus did, to cast out devils the way Jesus did. One woman, suffering from a blood disease, battled her way through a crowd just to touch the hem of Jesus' garment. One paralyzed man couldn't get to Jesus on his own, so his friends carried him to Jesus; and when they couldn't get into the building because of the crowds, they climbed up on the house, cut a hole in the roof, and lowered the man in to the room where Jesus was. That's how popular Jesus was at one time.

But later, when the winds of change had swept through the city of Jerusalem, and Jesus had gone from being the front-running messianic candidate to being just another convicted criminal, it was political suicide to be associated with him. You would risk the shame of being connected with a loser and of being ridiculed right along with him. For they hurled insults at him, they derided him, they mocked him with feigned pageantry as the type of king they saw him to be: a crown of thorns on his head, a purple garment covering his beaten and bloodied body, and in his hand a wilted reed for a scepter. And if you dared to align yourself with such a symbol of shame and derisive laughter, if you got too close, you too might be so tormented.

It's not the most popular thing in some circles to profess to be a believer in a created universe. It may cost you the professional esteem of your colleagues on the faculty or in the boardroom to profess the belief that a man could be killed and three days later rise again. You may get some funny looks from folks in the neighborhood when they learn that you believe that a figure from ancient history is still alive—as if you believe in Santa Claus or the Tooth Fairy. Am I the only one who's gone to a college reunion, told people that I belong to a Baptist church, and then watched their faces as they tried to hide their amusement? Some of us are couching our devotion to Christ in language that is more suitable or palatable to the modern culture. We refer to our spirituality instead of revealing that every now and then we fall to our knees and cry, "Holy is the Lord!" We talk about our meditation and reflection when what we really mean is "I prayed all night long, moaned all night long, sang all night long until I found the Lord." There are reasons why so many keep their distance from the cross of Christ.

And it wasn't just the shame and reproach of the cross; for some it was the physical inconvenience of such an undertaking. There were families to take care of and jobs to attend to. There was a Passover for those followers of Jesus, and they had to make ready, had to devote themselves to this important religious custom and family event. They were busy. The Sabbath was coming. They had things to do, places to go, people to see. Not everyone had the time to follow a condemned man as he trudged his way up to Golgotha carrying a heavy cross. And the weather had gone bad, stormy; darkness covered the land, and it looked like rain. It simply wasn't convenient to get outside the city walls just to watch a man die. We understand. We have better, more important things to do. Or maybe we worked the night shift or were up watching *The Late Late Show,* and we just were just too tired to get up and find our way to the foot of the cross. There are reasons why not everybody was there with Jesus when he gave his life as an atonement for sin.

I look at these four women in John 19:25, and I think to myself, "That's about the same number of people who show up for prayer meeting, who show up for midweek Bible study, who show up for those special programs on Sunday afternoons. Two thousand years of church history, and not much has changed. There are reasons why people were keeping their distance from Jesus, why they were staying away from him even after he had healed them, even after he had delivered them. John made a point in his Gospel of showing how each of Jesus' miracles was a sign that he was the Messiah. And yet, when it came to the sign of the cross, people were jeering him instead of cheering him—when the going got tough, most of them just got going. Apparently, all the blessings that he had bestowed on them were forgotten by the time Calvary came around. Apparently, the daily bread that he provided for them wasn't enough to keep them faithful to him. Apparently, the morning-by-morning new mercies that we see are not enough to elicit from us any real devotion, any real commitment, any zeal for who he is instead of just what he does. A song by Vicki Yoh'e insists on a worship of Christ that goes beyond what he's done: "Because of who you are I give you glory, because of who you are I give you praise. Because of who you are I will lift my voice and say, 'Lord, I worship you because of who you are.'"[1]

Closing the Gap

"Standing near the cross of Jesus were his mother, and his mother's sister, Mary the wife of Clopas, and Mary Magdalene." They were standing near the cross. And so while I fully comprehend the viewpoint of those who kept their distance—I've been one of them, having failed him from time to time—I wonder if there might be something for us as we contemplate the perspective of these who got a little closer to Jesus, those who were standing near the cross. "The closer I get to you," says the Roberta Flack song, "the more you make me see; by giving me all you got, your love has captured me."[2] And it's true: the closer I get to Jesus, the more closely I cling to him not just on Sunday but all week long, the more I realize how much he has done for me. Not just the miracles of days gone by, and not just the things that he's brought me through, but the love, the deep, deep love of Jesus—that's what impresses and captures me. He could have called thousands of angels to free him from the cross, but because he loves us, he remained there. He didn't have to take the punishment. He didn't have to endure the suffering. He didn't have to. His own words in the garden of Gethsemane reveal his hope that maybe he wouldn't have to face this gruesome death (Matthew 26:39). But because it was the only way to save us, redeem us, restore our relationship with God, he did it. He took the pain. He took the bruises, the stripes, the scorn, the mockery. He did it all for you and for me. And if you kept your distance, if you stayed away, if you refused to allow yourself to see that up close, you might well miss it. There are some things you can't see from a distance. There are some things you can't hear from a distance. There are some things you can't feel, you can't sense, you can't gather from a distance. If you keep your distance from Jesus, if you stay home from Bible study and prayer meeting, if you skip out on revival night and leave early from Sunday service, you might not appreciate how much he loves us.

And maybe that's what also compels us to keep our distance. We don't want to have a deep devotion to him. We don't want to fall in love with him. We don't want to be committed to him the way he is to us. We don't want to love him the way he loves us. And what a shame, what a tragedy, what a miscarriage of relational justice, that Jesus would love us with such a depth, such a power, such a strength, and we would do everything we can to keep our distance from him, to refuse to acknowledge how marvelous his love for us really is, to remain cold and empty inside simply because we are afraid to love. That's what the Roberta Flack song was about. It was a confession, an admission, that if we get too close, the revelation of love will capture us: "Over and over again I tried to tell myself that we could never be more than friends, but all the while, inside, I knew it was real—the way you make me feel."[3] The closer I get to Jesus, the more I realize who he is, the more he makes me see how much he loves me, the more he makes me feel his warm embrace, the more I understand the power of his love for me.

These women at the cross had a perspective that people who skip prayer meeting will never know. They had a commitment to Christ that we Sunday Christians have yet to achieve. They had a knowledge of Jesus that those of us who sleep in during Sunday school and skip out on midweek Bible study cannot get from the *Cliffs Notes* on him. They saw our Lord die. They saw our Lord suffer. They saw our Lord cut, bleeding, pierced, nailed to the cross, crying out to God in agony. They saw him thirst. They saw what no coward could perceive. They saw what no backslider could ever dare to imagine. They saw what no artist could ever properly render, what no song could ever adequately express, what no novel could ever sensibly articulate, what no movie could ever faithfully reproduce. They saw Jesus—Son of Man, Son of God, spotless Lamb of God slain from before the foundation of the world. They saw Jesus—the atonement for our sins, the lover of our souls, the rock of our salvation. They saw Jesus die for you and for me!

You can't see that and then return to business as usual. You can't understand what he did for us and then keep on acting like a fool. You can't know who Jesus really is and what he really did for us and remain the same. It has to change us. It must change us. The centurion who stood facing Jesus on the cross probably had never even heard of the man prior to that day, but even he, when he saw Jesus from that vantage point, from that close perspective, cried out, "Truly, this man was the Son of God!" (Mark 15:39).

God is calling us, through these women at the foot of the cross, to draw closer to Jesus. We must put away from our minds the busyness of American culture. We must set aside the agendas that we have established for ourselves that get in the way of our getting closer to Jesus. Let's not be preoccupied with what our colleagues or friends or neighbors will think of us if we get closer to Jesus. Let's rearrange our priorities, schedules, and lifestyles, and let's draw nearer to Jesus, nearer to his pierced hands and feet, nearer to his thorn-crowned brow, nearer to the crimson flow that for all sins was shed, nearer to his love, nearer to his mercy, nearer to his grace, nearer to his power, nearer to his sacrifice—nearer to our redemption.

Cross Examinations

1. What types of social pressure have you experienced that caused you to distance yourself publicly from your faith?
2. What excuses have you used for missing a worship service, Bible study, or other commitment to the church?

3. Has reading this book brought you closer to the cross of Christ? If so, how has that impacted your faith and/or your Christian walk?

Notes

1. Vicki Yoh'e, "Because of Who You Are," *I Just Want You* (Chordant, 2003).

2. Roberta Flack, "The Closer I Get to You," *Blue Light in the Basement* (Atlantic, 1977).

3. Ibid.

15

What Forgiveness Is Not
(Luke 23:23-38)

Then Jesus said, "Father,
forgive them; for they do not
know what they are doing."
(Luke 23:34)

The story of our Lord's death in the Gospels has many remarkable aspects. But no verse amazes and confounds me more than Luke 23:34, where Jesus says, "Father, forgive them." I have not found forgiveness to be anything like what a superficial reading of this verse seems to make it. And the history of human society has borne out that I'm not the only person who finds it difficult, often impossible, to forgive those who have injured us. Nations are at war with each other today because of events that occurred centuries and, in some cases, millennia earlier, because it is exceedingly difficult to forgive. And certainly if nations have difficulty forgiving, individuals are no different. This very day, as you read this, you may be wounded, spiritually bleeding, because of some blow dealt to you by someone you love, someone you trusted, someone you expected more of. And right now the very mention of forgiveness is beyond your ability to fathom. When we've been hurt by someone, we aren't thinking so much of forgiveness as of blame or retaliation or revenge, and sometimes of giving up altogether.

Here, however, is Jesus, face to face with his tormentors, making forgiveness look rather easy. How could he do that? How could he, the sinless Son of God, be crucified along with two common criminals? And then he forgives his executioners! It seems unjustifiable, unthinkable, unimaginable. But there it is.

Jesus, at the place called The Skull, between two criminals, battered, bruised, and bloodied, is dying a death that the Romans intended not only as a cruel punishment but also as a stern warning to anyone who would dare claim to be a king in a land ruled by Caesar. And yet, right then and there, he is seeking forgiveness for them. Incredible.

Recently I attended a conference on forgiveness run by the Council for Relationships for counselors, psychologists, and clergy. And from what I learned there about forgiveness, what Jesus did truly is unthinkable because, well, hardly anyone ever thinks of it! But also, over the course of time and acculturation we have essentially misunderstood and mischaracterized some things concerning forgiveness. And this misunderstanding and mischaracterization have prohibited many people from even entertaining the concept. In other words, many of us don't make anything near the effort at forgiveness that we ought to because we look at this particular story and saying and immediately decide that there is no way we can do what Jesus is doing. But what I'd like to amplify from this story, which is at the core of our faith, is the nature of Christ's forgiveness versus our concepts of it. Maybe, like me, you've had difficulty forgiving someone or you've been perplexed at someone's lack of forgiveness for you. In any event, let me start by challenging some of the wrong assumptions that many of us have about forgiveness, and perhaps then we will more capably deal with our own issues of reconciliation and also have a higher regard for what Jesus has done for us.

Forgiveness Takes Time

Forgiveness is not quick. And I believe that Christians may well have developed a false assumption about forgiveness being quick in large part from reading this verse, Luke 23:34, where Jesus, while still in the process of suffering at the hands of his tormentors, is already forgiving them. They're still taunting him, injuring him, gambling for his clothes. They will go on to pierce his side with a spear even after he had died, and already, before his tormentors had even stopped their abuse of him, he is forgiving them. And we find that too quick. If that's what forgiveness is, so quickly and readily offered even before the pain has subsided and the injuries are still being inflicted, then we don't want any part of it. It's too quick.

This is worth considering because some of us who have yet to recover from our wounds and are not quite ready to forgive think that we're falling far short of the standard that Jesus set for us. But we're not quite catching the whole story, for we're looking at Jesus in Luke 23, which in its literary context comes toward the end of the Gospel. And in its historical context, this chapter comes many hundreds of years after God made covenants with the patriarchs and Israel, covenants that God's people repeatedly and sinfully dishonored. And even far earlier, Adam and Eve sinned, breaking God's heart long before Luke ever wrote a word, long before the crowds demanded the release of Barabbas and the Roman soldiers treated Jesus so despicably. We may be looking only at the injuries recorded in Luke 23, but God, whose people had a long history of breaking the divine commandments, turning to other gods, and perverting justice, had been dealing with this issue for a long time.

Jesus on the cross was not the beginning of our sins, but the culmination of our redemption. Jesus on the cross was not a quickly assembled effort aimed at forgiveness for a few, but the historical climax of a long process aimed at forgiveness for all, ongoing since the time sin first entered the world, when God said to serpent, "I will put enmity between you and the woman, and between your offspring and hers; he will strike your head, and you will strike his heel" (Genesis 3:15). This forgiveness was a long time coming. This forgiveness of the debt of all our sins was painstakingly planned and carried out over many centuries. When Rahab turned on her own people and aided the Israelites, it was part of the forgiveness plan. When Ruth was widowed and brought to Israel with her mother-in-law Naomi, it was part of the forgiveness plan. When David and Bathsheba conceived Solomon, it was part of the forgiveness plan. And when the fullness of time had come, after forty-two generations had passed, when God finally was ready, then, as the Bible says, God "gave his only Son, so that whoever believes in him may not perish but have eternal life" (John 3:16).

Forgiveness takes time. We may feel the need to initiate the process of forgiveness, but if you find yourself struggling to give it to someone who needs it, or if you're wondering why someone whom you offended hasn't offered it to you yet, remember: forgiveness takes time.

Forgiveness Takes Repentance

Forgiveness is not the condoning of an offense. And indeed, some of us hesitate to forgive for fear that we may unintentionally be enabling the offender to continue the injurious behavior. It is the trend among some churches to proclaim a gospel without repentance, good news without change, salvation that doesn't actually save anyone from anything. Many Christians, especially some preachers, are more concerned about offending people than they are about helping people get reconciled with God. And when we look at injurious acts in our own lives, we know that we don't want to enable people to continue their hurtful behavior toward us. But somehow, when it comes to their relationship with God, some people think that it's all right to just keep on doing whatever it was that separated them from God in the first place. We look at this verse and perhaps say to ourselves, "Well, Jesus forgives me, so I'll keep on doing it." Paul had no time for that line of reasoning: "What then are we to say? Should we continue in sin in order that grace may abound? By no means!" (Romans 6:1). If he were alive here and now, Paul, instead of "By no means," might say, in the words of Fred Sanford, "Are you crazy?"

Let me be clear about something: I'm not slipping into a message of salvation by works. Jesus died on the cross so that, as Paul said, "By grace you have been saved through faith, and this is not your own doing; it is the gift of God—not the result of works, so that no one may boast" (Ephesians 2:8-9). Jesus said, "Father, forgive them; for they do not know what they are doing," so nothing that we have done or even will do would keep us from being reconciled to our heavenly Father. But if we think that this great forgiveness is a condoning of the actions that we commit that so injure our God, if we think that we have a license to sin because we have a merciful and gracious Father, if we think that he affirms the evil we commit, we are terribly mistaken. Forgiveness is not about condoning, but about atoning. Jesus didn't die to leave us in our sins, but to save us from our sins. He didn't lift us up out of the miry clay just to drop us right back into it.

I once heard the testimony of a young man who said that he had been totally lost, doing drugs, rebelling in any and every way he could. But when Jesus found him, when he heard that old, old story of Jesus and his love, when he came to the Lamb of God just as he was, all of a sudden he didn't want to rebel the way he used to. He didn't want to get high on drugs anymore. He was totally changed. Only a second chance can do that. Only forgiveness of sin and a realization that nothing can separate us from the love of God can do that. Only Jesus can do that.

Forgiveness Takes Work

Forgiveness is not easy. And again, if we look only at Luke 23:34, we may get a wrong impression about forgiveness, because all we see there is Jesus offering forgiveness. But what the wider literary context reveals is that Jesus went through an awful lot in order to offer that forgiveness to us. Before he could say those words of forgiveness that throughout all history he had been destined to say, he had to be betrayed by one of his own disciples, denied by another, and abandoned to his fate by the rest of them. Before he could say those words, he had to be falsely accused by false witnesses and convicted of false charges. Before he could say those words, he had to be mocked and spat upon, beaten and slapped, bloodied with whips and crowned with thorns, and nailed to a cross. All this was for sins that he didn't do, crimes that he hadn't committed. The hymn writer Isaac Watts pondered this and wrote, "Was it for crimes that I had done he groaned upon the tree? Amazing pity, grace unknown, and love beyond degree!"

There's no way around it: forgiveness isn't easy. Forgiveness is not for the faint of heart. Forgiveness takes some work, crying, and doubting, some dark days and long nights. But forgiveness is amazing. Forgiveness is redemptive. Forgiveness is our great hope for reconciliation with God our Father. Forgiveness is our hope for restored relationships, marriages, and families. Forgiveness is our hope for reconciliation among races and between nations. Forgiveness is our hope for peace on earth. Because "All have sinned and fall short of the glory of God" (Romans 3:23), and yet, "The LORD has laid on him the iniquity of us all" (Isaiah 53:6). And Jesus said, "Father, forgive them; for they do not know what they are doing."

I am so glad that God took the time and the pain to forgive me. I'm so grateful that God didn't get weary of me, didn't give up on me, didn't forget about me. I'm so thankful that God didn't just condone my sinful past but instead gave me a second chance to change and get it right. I don't even like to think about where or what I'd be right now if God had given up on me, if God hadn't taken the time, gone through the pain, kept alive the hope.

Jesus hasn't given up on you either. Maybe you think you've done something for which you can never be forgiven. But Jesus was praying about you when he said, "Father, forgive. . . ." You can have a second chance. You can be restored. You can be redeemed. You can have a fresh start. You can have it all tossed out and wiped away. Jesus came to forgive you and offer you that fresh start. It won't be quick, it won't be condoning what you've done, and it most definitely won't be easy. But it will be life-changing and life-giving.

Cross Examinations

1. How do you respond when others won't forgive you?
2. Who are the people whom you've had difficulty forgiving? Why?
3. What makes forgiving others difficult for you?
4. How does Christ's forgiveness of you affect your forgiveness of others?

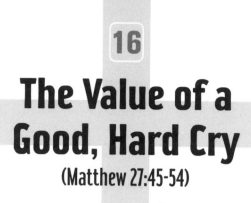

16

The Value of a Good, Hard Cry
(Matthew 27:45-54)

> About three o'clock Jesus cried with a loud voice, "Eli, Eli, lema sabachthani?" that is, "My God, my God, why have you forsaken me?" (Matthew 27:46)

There he was, the Lord of creation, the King of kings, the Lion of the tribe of Judah, the one who drove out demons, calmed storms, and conquered Lazarus's grave—nailed to a cross, bleeding, wounded, beaten, and defeated. And in the ultimate sign of weakness, Jesus cried. What an unimaginably dreadful experience it must have been that our Lord, in such deep agony and despair, and having no other recourse, would cry out, "My God, my God, why have you forsaken me?" And this scenario, because it is a part of redemption's story, indicates that there was and is value in the cries of our magnificent Savior.

Crying to Communicate

We mostly associate crying with babies. And for babies, crying is communicating. Crying is the most important way babies have of making their needs known to their parents. Some of us get so familiar with the different cries of a baby that we can tell exactly what the baby is trying to express—for example, hunger, pain, fear, or, all too often, the need for a clean diaper. The value of their loud cries is that they are communicating in the only way they know how.

When the doctor spanked my firstborn and she let out a cry, it communicated to me that she was alive and breathing. And that let me know that I could breathe again! Crying communicates things.

Crying as a means of communication has the effect of uncovering or revealing what might previously have been hidden and uncommunicated. In our society, crying is widely perceived as a sign of weakness, an act of the frail and the pathetic. *Babies* cry; we're adults, grownups, big people. "Never let them see you cry" goes the saying. It's like blood in the water for some folks: they'll think that you're weak and will take advantage of you. Well, many times we fall into the trap of being preoccupied with what people will think of us, when in reality what really concerns us is not so much what people will think but what they will know. It isn't that they'll think that we're weak; they'll know it. It isn't that God will think that we're sinners; God knows it. It isn't that folks will think that we're incapable of sustaining ourselves, but that we'll be forced to admit that we can't make it on our own.

A good, hard cry does not create our weakness, but it may well reveal to us that we are weak, that we need help. When the apostle Paul realized that he was weak, he said, "When I am weak, then I am strong" (2 Corinthians 12:10), because God had told him, "My power is made perfect in weakness." If we would really be strong, then, not just purporting to be so, not just acting like it, not just talking tough, we must first admit to being weak so that Christ can make us strong. What do I mean? If you never admit you need a doctor, you might be missing out on the cure for your disease. If you never admit that you love someone, you might never receive that person's love in return. The Bible puts it this way, "If we confess our sins, he who is faithful and just will forgive us our sins and cleanse us from all unrighteousness" (1 John 1:9). Weakness, admission, and confession lead to forgiveness and righteousness. Are you strong, intelligent, and secure, and do you not need anyone else? Really? Or are you hiding your weaknesses with a brave exterior? A good, hard cry might be the only way to make things happen and get you exactly what it is that you really need.

One author told about how her two teenage children, a son and a daughter, were sitting with her in the living room to watch a family friend model her wedding gown for them. And as the young bride-to-be came out into the living room magnificently adorned, radiating beauty and love, the mother began to cry and smile at the joy and hope of her friend. But her teenage daughter jumped up from the sofa and ran from the room in tears, shocking everyone. This teenage girl had been hiding her feelings of inadequacy, that she wasn't pretty enough, that her hair was too curly and her body too heavy. Maybe the boys weren't calling her, and the girls were teasing her. This is a significant concern among young people; they want to have a positive self-image, to like themselves. Far too many of them go about their lives feeling that they aren't good enough because they don't look like Britney Spears or Justin Timberlake, or they get no calls for dates, or the coaches and fans don't rave about their athletic prowess. And in that moment, supposedly focused on the bride-to-be, the tears of that teenage daughter revealed a poor self-image and self-disdain that otherwise might not have been known. Those tears of pain and hurt were what Janis Ian depicted so accurately in her daringly honest song "At Seventeen," where she wrote about how "Those of us with ravaged faces, lacking in the social graces, desperately remained at home, inventing lovers on the phone who called to say, 'Come dance with me.'"[1]

And it's not just teenagers who silently suffer within. There are many people, young and old, male and female, who go about hiding their hurts until something is said, something is done, some song is sung, some play is acted, some sermon is preached that resonates within their soul, that evokes an emotional release of crying that reveals what has been hidden for so long. Without those tears, those who love you best might never know what suffering you endure, how their love has missed the mark, or how the devil has played with your silence and fears and twisted them into a self-destructive low self-image that is spiraling you toward defeat. And sometimes until you cry, they might never know what lies beneath the surface, that you have a true need for friendship, love, and praise. That teenage girl who broke down at the sight of the bride-to-be had a loving mother and brother who affirmed her value, who praised her beauty, who lauded her worth. And some ten years later, when she stood in that same living room modeling her own wedding gown for her mother and brother, tears flowed again, but this time tears of joy. There is a value in a good, hard cry.

Crying for Help

From the cross of Calvary, Jesus cried out not only in communicating to his Father, but also at times in an urgent appeal for help. And indeed, sometimes people don't respond to a desperate situation without hearing a cry for help. My family recently had a reunion. Family reunions can sometimes be an exercise in trying to show everyone how well you're doing—pulling up in an expensive new car works well. Or you can get critical of others—one of your cousins has gained a lot of weight. But this time, there was a moment at the concluding worship experience when we prayed for each of the ten siblings of my father's generation and for their families. And one by one, prayer by prayer, we were moved by the emotions of each family's experiences. First there was my uncle Isaias's family, who were dealing with the death of a patriarch and missed him terribly. Then there was uncle Joe's family and my cousin who was being called up to active duty in Iraq. Then there were two families with children who had devastating diseases. For each family we prayed, and we cried long and hard. During the rest of the week we had been putting up façades of strength, but prayer time produced some desperate cries for help. My cousin Moises, a preacher whose son was born with autism, asked us to pray for a miracle for his son, and for a miracle for my brother Jonathan's son who was born with a rare and debilitating disease that doctors say is incurable. Moises lifted up his tear-filled voice and led us in a prayer that was half desperation and half inspiration, and that left us all crying out to the Lord, sensing the pain of these parents and grandparents and siblings, and grasping at the only deliverance available to us, through the power of prayer.

Have you been there? Maybe not with those particular needs, but have you been in dire straits in some situation of your own, where prayer was all that was left to you? You've tried everything, been to every doctor, consulted every counselor, squeezed every last penny out of your budget, until there was nothing left available to you but to lift up your voice and cry out to the Lord in prayer: "My God, help me!" There are psalms in the Bible written especially to communicate that kind of sentiment, that emotion. David wrote of how he cried unto the Lord with his voice, and the Lord delivered him from all his fears: "In my distress I called upon the LORD; to my God I cried for help. From his temple he heard my voice, and my cry to him reached his ears" (Psalm 18:6).

Our Scripture text tells us that while Jesus was dying on the cross, while he was doing exactly what God had called him to do, he too cried out with a loud voice. He too cried out as David did a thousand years before, "My God, my God why have you forsaken me?" (Psalm 22:1). He too was emotionally wounded by the feeling that God hadn't answered his prayers, that God hadn't delivered him from his physical suffering. From this we can take comfort that Jesus knows what we're going through. Jesus cried out just like you and I cry out. He too was doing what he should be doing, and yet everything seemed to go wrong. He too did not deserve the fate that befell him. He too wanted to sense that God was still in control, that the arc of the moral universe was still bending toward justice. And he too cried out loud in prayer. Jesus has been there.

The Response to Crying

Not only does crying communicate what might have been hidden and issue a desperate appeal for help, but also it prompts a response from the hearer. I've grown fond of Psalm 116 because the psalmist speaks of his cry to the Lord from the vantage point of the past tense, telling the whole story of what happens for us when we cry out to the Lord. He said, "I love the LORD, because he has heard my voice and my supplications. Because he inclined his ear unto me, therefore I will call on him as long as I live" (Psalm 116:1-2). I love the Lord today, and I'm not ashamed to say so. I've cried to the Lord, and the Lord has heard me and brought me a mighty long way. Crying as a means of communication oftentimes prompts a response. There is a value in a good, hard cry.

I'm reminded of my father-in-law's conversion story. He was a little boy when he gave his heart to the Lord, and the Lord saved him. He went home that day and told his brothers and sisters that he had been saved. And they ridiculed him and said, "How do you know you were saved?" And he said, "Because I cried." They replied, "That doesn't mean anything. You cry for everything!" He answered, "Yeah, but this time I liked it."

Matthew tells us, "Jesus cried again with a loud voice and breathed his last" (Matthew 27:50). And from that moment on, things began to happen. The curtain of the temple was torn, the earth shook, rocks were split, tombs were opened and saints were raised from death. And when a centurion and those with him saw all this, when they watched the Lord suffer and cry out until he couldn't cry any more, they were terrified and said, "Truly this man was God's son!" (Matthew 27:54). I wonder if you've ever looked at Jesus suffering on the cross for us and been moved to tears, moved to repentance, moved to admitting that we were wrong and Jesus was right. Have you ever paused to notice the cries of Jesus as the centurion and his companions did that day?

I can describe the effect of Jesus' cries on the centurion by telling about how my family was sitting around the kitchen one day when I was in my early teens. My mother was cooking dinner, having already put in a full day's work at her job. And I don't know who set it off, but it could have been any of us who complained about the dinner menu that night. "Why do we have to have that? We always eat that. I don't like it anyway. Why can't we order out?" You know what I'm describing, and it wasn't all that unusual. But that night, my mom blew up. And I don't mean in a "Now you kids are gonna get it!" kind of way, but she lost it. She broke down and started crying, shaking and sobbing right there at the stove. Through her tears she cried out, "You guys don't appreciate all that I do for you. You just sit there and complain. You don't offer to help. I work all day and come home and do my best for you for dinner, and this is what you do?" I was changed that night. And as a family, we grew up that night. No more taking for granted all that our mother was doing for us. No more acting like spoiled brats, complaining when we didn't get what we wanted, acting up when things didn't go our way, when all the while mom was doing her best, working her hardest, loving us with all she had.

What do the tears of Jesus mean to you? Do you hear his cries and understand that he was doing it all for you and for me? Do they move you to finally understand his great love for us? Do his loud cries at last turn our ungrateful hearts and complaining mouths into sources of praise and adoration for all the great things that he has done? Do they? Or do we go yet unmoved by his cries, standing there doing nothing, never noticing all that he did, never acknowledging all that he went through, all that he endured for you and for me, for your salvation and mine?

Do you ever ask yourself, along with the great hymnist Isaac Watts, "Was it for crimes that I had done he groaned upon the tree? Amazing pity, grace unknown, and love beyond degree!"? Did he cry out for me? Was it my fault? Were those my sins, my rebellion, my pride that led him to cry so loud and long on that cross? When he cried out, "Father, forgive them; for they do not know what they are doing" (Luke 23:34), was I the one he had on his mind?

What value do Jesus' cries have for you? Today, if you hear his voice, do not harden your heart. Listen. Respond.

Cross Examinations

1. How do you deal with your weaknesses?
2. How has prayer impacted your moments of weakness?
3. What impact has Jesus' dying for your sins had on your life? What impact should it have?

Note

1. Janis Ian, "At Seventeen," *Between the Lines* (Sony Music Entertainment, 1975).

17

God's View of Golgotha
(Matthew 27:55-61)

Many women were also there, looking on from a distance; they had followed Jesus from Galilee and had provided for him. (Matthew 27:55)

Just outside the doors of my church's worship space, in the newly renovated foyer, are four remarkable paintings that came from the soul and brush of a beloved member and friend, Lucien Crump. I can't say that one is more striking than the other, because each has its own place of ministry in the hearts and lives of our church members. But one painting portrays what I imagine Lucien had in mind for God's view of Jesus' death that Friday just outside the walls of Jerusalem on Golgotha's hill. It's an aerial view that depicts the descent from the cross, how our slain Lord's broken body was taken down. Lucien painted a rather tall, upright view from the ground of that same scene. It was my favorite, and he knew it. He made a smaller version of it that hangs in my home along with several other images that he created. But this descent from the cross, this aerial view in our foyer, reminds me that God was watching over Jesus, and that God was watching over those who would be faithful to him. So just in case my church thinks that God isn't paying attention to our fickle church-attendance patterns, to our inconsistent level of volunteer work, to our holding back of the tithe or skimping on mission support, or any other number of ways that we are not doing right by God's Son, Lucien's painting reminds us that God has a good view of what we're doing.

Each of the four Gospels mentions that there were women who remained as close to Jesus as they could throughout his ordeal. Our text says that they had followed Jesus from Galilee and had provided for him. And God was watching them. Galilee, where Jesus was from—that's where he performed many miracles, where he healed Peter's mother-in-law, where he walked on the water, where he calmed a raging sea, where he taught the masses. These women had followed him from Galilee. And they had a whole lot more company with them when they were in Galilee. In Galilee, all kinds of folks were following Jesus. In Galilee, they were lining up to get in to see him. In Galilee, when they couldn't get in the front door, they'd climb up on the housetop, cut a hole in the roof, and lower the sick into the room below to get close to Jesus. In Galilee, there were huge crowds of those who would follow Jesus. It was the place to be. It was the thing to do. It was fashionable. It was trendy. It was cool to follow Jesus, the miracle worker from Galilee.

But come to Jerusalem, come to Pilate's courtyard, come to the road to Golgotha, come to Calvary's hill, and instead of crowds cheering for Jesus, it's Barabbas they want freed, and Jesus they want crucified. And as for his supporters, it's like the lone grateful leper of the ten cured—hardly anyone was there to stand up for Jesus. The prophetic words that Jesus recalled were right on the money: smite the shepherd, and the sheep will be scattered. Our human fickleness is nowhere more clearly displayed than here. Our drive for success and our determination to be victorious, our front-running nature whereby we jump on the bandwagon with whomever is leading the pack—that's what's so prominently exhibited. In fact, by the time evening was approaching and Jesus' body hung grotesquely nailed to that wooden cross, the presence of the women is remarkable: there were still some followers who had not stopped following, some supporters who had not stopped supporting, some believers who had not stopped believing. And God was watching the entire spectacle.

I wonder if we ever ponder seriously that God is watching us, not just when we're alone and no one else sees us, but also when we're in public, when we're quite aware that people are watching, and we have a choice to behave either how they might want us to act or how God calls us to act. Are we cognizant of the reality that there is a God in heaven who sits high but who looks low, even when everybody is doing it, even when we would just be one of the many who think that it's cool to "diss" Jesus, to hate him, to put him out of the public schools and the courtrooms, and out of the public venue altogether? What would happen if we were aware not only that everybody around us is watching us, but also that God is watching us as we forsake Christ's teachings, as we forget about how we were raised in Sunday school, as we betray our upbringing and betray God's Word and Son. In chapter 8 we looked at how Pilate, even though he knew that Jesus was innocent, handed him over to be crucified as the masses wished. How many times have we forsaken Christ because we were aware that everybody else was watching us? And what would our actions have been if we had been cognizant of the fact that God also is watching? Whom are we trying to please?

The Mistreatment of God's Son

Lucien Crump's painting reminds us that God was watching that scene on Golgotha's hill that day. What did God see? First, God watched people horribly mistreat his Son. God was watching it then, and God is watching it now. It must have horrified God the Father to watch how humanity would mistreat his only begotten Son. I can hardly watch when one of my daughters skins a knee, so I can't even imagine what it would be like to see all humanity turn on my children and mock them, spit on them, and torture them, laughing all the while. But that's what God saw.

God is watching every bomb and bullet that tears the bodies of the people of Iraq. God is watching every act of abuse that takes place in military prisons around the world. God is watching every brutal governmental leader involved in the starvation and genocide in Darfur. God is watching every politician who stands idly by while students in our inner cities work in dilapidated buildings and are victimized by drug dealers and gangs in the schoolyards. God is watching! It's popular nowadays to talk about God helping those who help themselves, and about people pulling themselves up by their bootstraps, but as Jesus said, whenever we look the other way and fail to help "the least of these," we fail him (Matthew 25:31-46). When Pilate gave in to the will of the people and their selfish, hateful, and murderous desires, when they tortured and beat and pierced our Lord Jesus, God was watching. "Inasmuch as you have done it to the least of these, you have done it unto me." God is watching.

Faithfulness to God's Son

God also witnessed the faithfulness of the women and of Joseph of Arimathea. And there are two different stories here. The women followed Jesus in the good times and in the bad times. Their fidelity was unwavering. Their love was loyal and true. Whether people were singing "Hosanna!" or shouting "Crucify him!" these women were faithful. Joseph, on the other hand, was a member of the religious establishment, someone who had a voice in the matter. And when Jesus was performing miracles in Galilee and the Sanhedrin was condemning him, looking for a way to trip him up, Joseph had stayed silent. It wasn't politically expedient for him to stand up for Jesus at that time, and so he remained silent to cover his political backside. But when the Sanhedrin actually took up the issue of condemning Jesus to death, when they proposed a course of action that would lead to Jesus being crucified like a common criminal, when they devised a plan to lie about Jesus, to produce false witnesses, to lie to Pilate about who Jesus was and what he had done, Joseph stood up for the Lord. Luke reports that Joseph had not consented to their plan (Luke 23:50-51). He objected. He stood up.

There was a time when Joseph was not standing up, when he was weak in his discipleship, ashamed of the Lord Jesus Christ. Of course, nobody does the right thing all the time, but what do we do when the chips are down, when the pressure is on, when push comes to shove? Will we stand up for Jesus and be counted? Joseph wasn't perfect, but he stood up. He'd blown it before, but he stood up. He hadn't always had the faith to stand up for Jesus, but he was willing at the cross, willing when the chips were down. It's one thing to vote behind closed doors, but it's another to put public opinion aside and do what you can for the Lord. And though it was socially damning for him to identify himself with a convicted and executed criminal, Joseph of Arimathea joined with the women in standing up for Jesus. And since he had the means, he did what he could for his slain Savior and Lord. He used his power and connections to persuade Pilate to let him have Jesus' body. He used his own means to provide a new tomb, and he laid the body of the Lord there. Whatever he had, he was giving it up to Jesus. And God was watching that too.

God sees your labor for Jesus Christ. God sees you working in the kitchen of the church. God sees you reaching out to the hungry and the homeless. God sees you giving generously to others and wants you to know that your labor is not in vain. God wants you to know that what you do for Christ is appreciated and will endure. Even if no one else sees, if no one else thanks you, if no one else appreciates your service, if no one else pays attention to what you've done for Christ, God is watching you. And one of these days, you will wear a crown. One of these days, you'll put on your long white robe. One of these days, the trumpet will sound, the dead in Christ will rise, and we who are alive and remain will be caught up together with them in the air. One of these days, you will have your reward. So it's all right now, because God is watching you. God is telling you, in the words of the apostle Paul, "Be steadfast, immovable, always excelling in the work of the Lord, because you know that in the Lord your labor is not in vain" (1 Corinthians 15:58). God is watching you.

The Death of God's Son

Finally, and what I gather was most prominent in God's view of that scene, was not the mistreatment of God's Son by his tormentors, and not even the faithfulness and devotion shown to him by the women and Joseph of Arimathea, but rather the sight of an only child dying. For any parent, that agonizing experience would overshadow all else. The difference here, however, is that this death was God's own idea, God's own plan. God was the one who said that the serpent would bruise the heel of Eve's seed. God was the one who said that another deliverer like Moses would arise. God was the one who set in motion a plan of redemption that spanned forty-two generations, culminating in the virgin birth of Jesus: "For a child has been born for us, a son given to us; authority rests upon his shoulders; and he is named Wonderful Counselor, Mighty God, Everlasting Father, Prince of Peace" (Isaiah 9:6).

Why? What prompted God to do all this? What was it that kept God the Father from sending thousands of angels to save his Son from the agony of the cross? Jesus said it best in his discourse with Nicodemus: "For God so loved the world, that he gave his only begotten Son; that whosoever believeth in him should not perish, but have everlasting life" (John 3:16 KJV). God let it happen and watched it unfold out of love for us. God allowed his Son, who knew no sin, to become sin for us. God watched as his only Son took our penalty, took our punishment, took our pain and our chastisement. All of it is because God loves us, wants to be reconciled with us, for all his children to come together one day. If you remember nothing else from this paragraph, chapter, or book, please remember this: God loves you. God is watching, and he loves you. God knows that you've rebelled, messed up, failed to do what's right, mistreated his Son. God knows all of it. And God wants you to know that he loves you.

Cross Examinations

1. How have you mistreated or misused God's gifts to you?
2. Whom do you see being faithful to Christ the way these women and Joseph were faithful to him at Calvary?
3. In what ways do you observe the love of God in your life?

18

A Constant Reminder

(John 20:19-29)

After he said this, he showed
them his hands and his side.
(John 20:20)

The thrill of victory is an overwhelming feeling. One of the best sports films of all time is *Hoosiers*.[1] In one scene, a little-used player who sits at the end of the bench gets pressed into service at the end of a game. He turns the ball over, shoots an airball, and then gets fouled and has to make two free throws to win the game. With the whole town praying nervously, he goes up to the line and sinks two in a row. Afterward, when the press is interviewing him, instead of a scared and jittery kid who was certain he wouldn't make two free throws, a cool and cocky kid tells the reporter, "Oh, I knew I had it all the way." Somehow, in the splendor of victory, in the rush of excitement that floods the souls of victors everywhere, some things tend to get lost.

In John 20, where the amazing story of the resurrection of the crucified Lord is told, there is a color throughout the writing that seeps through the rejoicing of the text, first in John 20:9, when Peter and the Beloved Disciple did not understand the Scripture "that he must rise from the dead," and later in John 20:11, when Mary stood weeping. But mainly and most profoundly it is in John 20:20, when Jesus, after he had appeared to all the disciples and stood among them, showed them his hands and his side. Right then, in that instant, after having their highest hopes realized, experiencing their greatest triumph that their crucified

Lord was alive again, that victory had been snatched from the jaws of defeat, that everything was going to be all right, Jesus displayed for them his constant reminder of what it took for that moment of unequaled joy to have come about. He showed them his hands and his side.

Any tendency that we might have to underestimate the scarring of our Lord will be challenged a few verses later when John divulges that those scars were deep enough that someone could put a finger in the holes in Jesus' hands, and place a hand in the hole in his side (John 20:27). Nails had been driven through those hands; a spear had pierced that side. It must have been quite a moment for the disciples, when two extreme but cooperating emotions converged into one. The jubilation of the presence of the risen Savior combined with the shock and pain of seeing his wounds. The sight of those wounds that evening, the sight of his hands and his side still deeply marked with the signs of Golgotha's cruelty, had to become a constant reminder of what Jesus had endured for our sins.

I mentioned in chapter 6 that on March 27, 2005, the membership of the church that I pastor celebrated Easter Sunday worship in its newly renovated facility. The excitement at the church that week was contagious, and everyone in the congregation was a little delirious with "renovationitis." But that enthusiasm wasn't something that we all had at first. In fact, some didn't want to go through the renovation process at all. After a few asbestos findings and other problems, I wasn't sure that there were any true believers left. But when the work was done, it led to that sense of excitement that everyone in the church experienced.

After announcing in the midweek e-mail before Easter Sunday that we would indeed be worshiping in the sanctuary that Sunday, I received several e-mails in return. One said, "This is really exciting stuff." Another person wrote, "I can't wait to have Sunday school in our new building." And a new member really got swept away, saying, "This is great! I love this church!" And personally, well, I was just about doing cartwheels in the sanctuary! Yet, when we were preparing the facility, hanging up Lucien Crump's marvelous paintings of the Passion and crucifixion in prominent places, I was startled, indeed shocked, by his works of art that provided such vivid reminders of what this is all about.[2] And then, one afternoon as I was walking through the building resuming my prayer routine, I came from the back of the sanctuary and turned toward the front, and I stopped to stare at the imposing, old rugged cross there. It was yet another constant reminder of what this is all about: Christ Jesus came to save sinners.

And then it's Easter, the celebration of the resurrection of our Lord. History does not record a more astonishing turn of events than that of Easter Sunday morning, when the angels proclaimed at Jesus' tomb, "He is not here; for he has been raised" (Matthew 28:6). Paul wrote, "If Christ has not been raised, then our proclamation has been in vain and your faith has been in vain" (1 Corinthians 15:14). But in fact, Paul continues, "Christ has been raised from the dead, the first fruits of those who have died," and "Death has been swallowed up in victory," so "Thanks be to God, who gives us the victory through our Lord Jesus Christ" (1 Corinthians 15:20,54,57).

When I was a child in my father's Pentecostal church, Easter was the best day of the year because that was when all the grown-ups would really praise the Lord. Everybody would "get happy" on Easter. Uncle Ed would start singing, "I know the Lord will make a way." Brother Ralph would start marching. Brother Louie would start dancing down the aisle like he had a pain in his back. And we kids loved it. And why not? Why not praise Jesus? Jesus is alive. Jesus changed them. Jesus made them brand new. These people had a relationship with Jesus, and they'd never be the same again. Why not praise him? Why not love him? Why not sing and shout the victory?

But then there's that twentieth verse of the twentieth chapter of John's Gospel. In the midst of the disciples' singing, praising, and marching, so to speak, Jesus showed them his hands and his side. I can only imagine the impact of that moment, the aim of Jesus' action in revealing this constant reminder forever embedded in his body. Why would he do that, and why did John record it for us years later? Why not cover Jesus' suffering and his wounds? Why provide them and us with that constant reminder?

Remember the Cost

First, Jesus showed them the wounds in his body because of the human propensity to forget the high price of salvation. Kids always think that money grows on trees. Youth think that parents owe them a car like the one the neighbor's kids got. And adults are no better. Look at the federal budget, and see how the president and Congress have spent billions on war seemingly without realizing that someone was going to have to pay for it, and then figuring that they could get some of the war funding by simply sacrificing programs and services that directly benefit the poor. In other words, make the poor pay for it. We tend to forget that life has costs, that blessings have a cost, that all these blessings come from someplace. And we certainly tend to forget the great sacrifice that yielded a resurrected Savior of our souls.

Dietrich Bonhoeffer wrote an amazing book, which every Christian ought to read more than once, called *The Cost of Discipleship*. "Cheap grace," he wrote, "is the deadly enemy of our church."[3] We take the grace of Christ for granted, as though it cost him nothing to save the world from its sins. Grace is indeed given freely to us, but if in our celebrations, festivals, and dedications we forget its great cost—the suffering and death of Christ—if we become proud and haughty, if we think of ourselves as better than others, if we lose all semblance of a life of service and become consumers of blessings instead of channels of blessings, then we need that constant reminder of the sacrifice and suffering that saved our souls. That's why Christians regularly partake of the Lord's Supper; that's why my church hung that cross to be so high and conspicuous in the worship space; that's why Lucien Crump painted his scenes of Christ's Passion: we tend to forget what Jesus did for you and for me.

Remember the Love

Jesus showed them his wounded body also because we need to know how much he loves us. I went home to my mom's house for the funeral of an uncle. At the meal after the evening wake service, my children and I had been awake at that point for about twenty-two straight hours. And my older daughter was brave. She made it all the way through the service but conked out at the meal. So I sat her next to my mom, put her head on the table, and told my mom to watch her for me while my younger daughter—the night owl—and I mingled. I kept looking across the room at my mom and my older daughter, and then my mom got up and walked away, leaving her there at the table asleep. So I figured that my mom would be right back, but I went over to the table anyway, just in case, to wait until she returned. About ten minutes went by, and mom never returned. And I couldn't see my dad anywhere either. So I took out my cell phone and called the house. My mom answered, and she was laughing.

I asked, "Why are you laughing?

She said, "Because we used to forget you under the pew all the time, and now we forgot not only you, but your family too!" Then she added, "Dad is on his way back to get you."

And I told her, "I love you, mom."

She said, "Why, because I always forget you?"

And I replied, "No, because you always come back for me."

How great is the love of our Savior for us. My wife likes to say that everybody needs a friend who is willing to go to jail for you. But how great a love is this that God the Father didn't spare his only Son for you and for me! How great is the Son's love for us that he gave his life for you and for me! We didn't deserve it. We were lost in our trespasses and sins. We were unfaithful, uncommitted, backsliding sinners. But God loves us so much. No price is too big. And if we see anything in the cross of Christ and in this Scripture about how Jesus showed them his hands and his side, let it be a clear vision that when Jesus says he loves us, he means it. That's what he was willing to do for me and for you.

Remember the Resurrection

Finally, Jesus showed the disciples that constant reminder of his hands and side also because those wounds were solid, irrefutable proof that reminded the disciples that he had indeed been dead, but now he is alive. And if he could do that, if he could overcome death, then he can overcome anything. No wonder he said, "All things can be done for the one who believes" (Mark 9:23). No wonder he said, "If you have faith the size of a mustard seed, you will say to this mountain, 'Move from here to there,' and it will move; and nothing will be impossible for you" (Matthew 17:20). No wonder Paul says, "My God will fully satisfy every need of yours according to his riches in glory in Christ Jesus" (Philippians 4:19).

If Jesus could overcome the wounds of whips on his back, the crown of thorns on his head, and the purple robe of mockery on his bloodied body, if he could overcome the jeering, taunting, and inhumanity heaped upon him, if he could overcome the *crucifixion* and the *grave,* then he can overcome anything. He can overcome racism. He can overcome weapons of mass destruction. He can overcome irreconcilable differences. He can overcome the strongest addictions. He can overcome our biggest failures. He can overcome our gravest sins. How did John put it later in one his letters? "The one who is in you is greater than the one who is in the world" (1 John 4:4).

The marks in Jesus' hands and side, the wounds in the body of the resurrected, victorious, all-powerful, all-loving Savior, are proof that nothing is too hard for God. No matter what you've done, no matter where you've been, no matter what you've seen, no matter where you are, Jesus is alive, and he can restore you to life too. Let those marks be a constant reminder: Jesus can do it!

Cross Examinations

1. What is an appropriate Christian attitude in light of the suffering that Jesus endured for our salvation?
2. How do you show love for those in your life?
3. What proof do you cite for believing in the lordship of Jesus Christ?
4. How has the hope borne out of the resurrection of Jesus Christ impacted your life? The lives of others around you?

Notes

1. *Hoosiers,* directed by David Anspaugh (MGM, 1986).

2. On Lucien Crump's paintings, see chapter 17.

3. Dietrich Bonhoeffer, "The Cost of Discipleship" in *A Testament to Freedom,* eds. Geffrey B. Kelly and F. Burton Nelson (San Francisco: Harper San Francisco, 1995), 307.